You Are Where You Eat

You Are Where You Eat

*Stories and Recipes from the
Neighborhoods of New Orleans*

Elsa Hahne

University Press of Mississippi / *Jackson*

www.upress.state.ms.us

Designed by Todd Lape

The University Press of Mississippi is a member
of the Association of American University Presses.

Copyright © 2008 by University Press of Mississippi
All rights reserved
Manufactured in Singapore

First printing 2008
∞
Library of Congress Cataloging-in-Publication Data

Hahne, Elsa.
  You are where you eat : stories and recipes from the
neighborhoods of New Orleans / Elsa Hahne.
     p. cm.
  Includes index.
  ISBN 978-1-57806-941-5 (cloth : alk. paper) 1. Cookery,
American—Louisiana style. 2. Cookery—Louisiana—New
Orleans. 3. Food habits—Louisiana—New Orleans. 4. Cookery,
International. I. Title.
  TX715.2.L68H327 2008
  641.59763—dc22   2008003699

British Library Cataloging-in-Publication Data available

To Patrick

Contents

Acknowledgments

Special thanks go out to Larissa Adriazola, Neil Alexander, David Beriss, George Aaron Broadwell, Jane Harvey Brown, Bethany Bultman, Richard Campanella, Heather Price Cooper, Crescent City Farmers Market, Dorignac's Food Center, Lolis Elie, Dan Etheridge, Mary Gehman, Craig Gill, Helen Gillet, John Green, Robert L. Hall, Gwendolyn Midlo Hall, John Kemp, Cecilia Kjellgren, Al Kleindienst, Langenstein's Supermarket, John Magill, Ryan Mattingly, Charles Mégnin, Jennifer Mitchel, Tom Morgan, Pamela Munro, Maida Owens, Jessie Perlik, Bruce Raeburn, Sally K. Reeves, Josephine Riccobono, Daryl Richard, Sara Roahen, Ama Rogan, Reine Pema Sanga, Ben Schenck, Rebecca Snedeker, Geneva "Gee" Mercadel-Tucker, Kip Sharpe, Harriet Swift, Nicole Taylor, Tamar Taylor, Susan Tucker, Malle Vogel, Elena Reeves-Walker, Laura Westbrook, Liz Williams, Cameron Wood, and all the people in this book who shared their recipes and stories.

This book has been made possible through grants from the Louisiana Endowment for the Humanities, a state affiliate of the National Endowment for the Humanities, as well as the New Orleans Jazz & Heritage Festival and Foundation, Inc.

Introduction

This is a book about home cooks in a city that is obsessed with cooking, eating, and talking about food. For natives and newcomers alike, New Orleans seems to inspire a heightened appreciation for the sensual experience of eating and drinking and for the skill of preparing food well. Even after the disasters of 2005, following hurricanes Katrina and Rita, it is still easier to strike up a conversation with a stranger about food than about the weather or what you do for a living. If you go to a party in New Orleans and ask someone enjoying a bowl of okra gumbo, "So what do you do?," you're likely to get an answer like "I roast my okra in the oven first, to get rid of the slime" instead of a business card. Standards are high. Home cooks have plenty to live up to here because each dish is lustily compared to similar fare savored in the past. Cooking for one's family takes skill and stamina, creativity coupled with a grasp of tradition, thick skin, and a certain bravado. Most of all, it takes lifelong devotion.

After making New Orleans my home in 2002, I was surprised to find that almost all the attention paid to local cooking was focused on restaurants, while more people seemed to cook at home every day in New Orleans than in any other place I had ever been. Restaurant cooking is a vital part of New Orleans cuisine, but many of the chefs and line cooks in New Orleans come from homes filled with great cooks who never worked, and rarely eat, in a restaurant. Grandmothers and uncles pass on cooking traditions that are so much part of daily life here that they almost pass unnoticed until a food critic *discovers* them in a French Quarter restaurant, hidden under cream sauces, red wine reductions, and trend ingredients du jour, looking like something out of *Gourmet* magazine.

Home cooks rarely consider what they do as art, but they nevertheless contribute immensely through their everyday cooking to the culinary artistry and cultural wealth of New Orleans. They keep their families and communities together with food, and entire neighborhoods continue to build and rebuild around kitchens. Many of the home cooks in this book do what could be called "open door cooking." If you dropped by their house right now, you would probably be given a plate of food because they always have something on the stove or in the refrigerator to serve anyone who comes to their door, whether it's Monday or Sunday.

For the purposes of this book, my criterion for a home cook is that the person cooks at home. Of course, but what else? I chose people who are not professionally trained but learned to cook from family members, friends, neighbors, and books, as well as through trial and error. Many of them regularly pull their dinner out of the waters and swamps inside and outside greater New Orleans, because hunting and fishing remain important to city life.

When I interviewed these home cooks, I brought a microphone and a recorder and tried to ask as few questions as possible. I literally got more than I asked for. Some people were so used to talking about food that I quickly realized I wasn't the first guest who had been invited to their buffet of memories. Others had to simmer for a while before they were ready to serve me something. Eventually, through all of these cooking stories, I began to learn about the history of the different neighborhoods, residential patterns, ethnic diversity, economic differences, family relationships, social infrastructure, and race relations, as well as the meaning of community and home. People described their hopes, dreams, and deepest memories in terms of food. Cooking plays such a fundamental role in their lives that some of them could not bring themselves to talk to me until they were out of their Katrina trailers and into their own kitchens again.

I interviewed more than a hundred home cooks from 2004 to 2007 knowing that only about thirty were going to fit into this book. Deciding whom to include was very difficult. This could have been a book about a thousand people. Fabulous cooks were left out because their stories were too similar or because they simply were not able to express themselves in words. I knew from the start that I wanted everyone to speak for himself or herself, making this book a collection of first-person accounts. If I had described each person and told their stories for them, this book would not have been nearly as rich. I wanted you to hear their voices.

Another reason I arrived at this selection of people was that I wanted to represent as many of the different neighborhoods as possible, as well as a number of the groups that historically have shaped and continue to shape New Orleans history, such as French, African, Native American, and Spanish in the beginning; Irish and German in the mid-1800s; Italian (Sicilian, really) around the year 1900; and more recently Latino and Vietnamese. Some groups that I would have liked to represent are not here because of lack of time or lack of luck. My overarching goal was to have this book show such diversity that all the home cooks in New Orleans would be able to find someone on these pages to identify with and a story they could relate to and recognize. All the people you meet here live in the city or one of the neighboring parishes. They are not close personal friends of mine, but they are fabulous home cooks and storytellers. I met them through community and neighborhood organizations, churches and schools, festivals, and friends of friends.

Following each interview I developed an intimate relationship with the pause button on my recorder as I transcribed verbatim everything that was said about food. Then began the agony of chopping hours and hours of stories down to about eight hundred words. Rich anecdotes and satisfying detail had to be cut in order to concentrate the flavor and improve the flow of each piece. It felt like fasting while I was seated at a feast. Often, I had to cut things that came up in several interviews in order to make the pieces shorter, while the sheer repetition of certain stories would have made it clear that different people in New Orleans often share the same experiences when it comes to cooking and eating.

As a case in point, practically everyone in this book makes red beans and rice. Most of them make gumbo. Red beans and rice and gumbo are emblematic of New Orleans food, and rightly so. Strangers on the street in New Orleans (go ahead—ask!) have at least some idea of what does or does not go into the pot.

In the final stages of editing this book, I visited a graduate class in geography at Tulane University to speak about my project. Only one student had been born in New Orleans. The other fifteen or so had come here to complete their studies. Picture this. Born in New Orleans? One hand in the air. Fix red beans and rice? Ten hands, with proudly wiggling fingers. Eating and cooking New Orleans foods is such an intrinsic part of local culture that one doesn't truly arrive here until there is something simmering on the stove. The first time I made a passable gumbo it felt like a graduation. Similarly, Katrina exiles in every other city in America continue to cook New Orleans food in an attempt to feel at home, while locals in FEMA trailers don't feel at home at all because they cannot cook the large amounts they used to. Trailers, which were supposed to provide temporary housing after the storm, have become semipermanent dwellings for people who've had to wait for money from insurance companies and the government, as well as for permits and for political decisions to be made.

Hurricane Katrina devastated many lives in New Orleans. The portraits in this book, however, testify to the strength and survival of life here, built around friends, family, and food. Aida, Avery, Bertin, Bill, Chin, Estella, Marietta, Peter, and Snježana were interviewed for the first time before the storm, whereas everyone else you meet here was interviewed after. Not everyone mentioned Katrina in the later interviews. Some, like Thania and Karen, did. Of all the people I interviewed before the storm, only two do not live in New Orleans today (neither of them is in this book). The people I interviewed are probably not representative of the general population, since many New Orleanians never came back or moved away soon after Katrina. Why didn't these home cooks stay away? One possible explanation is that big cooking and strong communities go together and feed one

another. Right after the storm, I must admit, I was deeply worried about whether people would actually return. But they did. And they're here now, pans flying.

I should say something about the recipes in this book. Part of me wanted to publish them as oral histories, which is how many of them came to me. Most of these home cooks never think of what they do in recipe form or see the point of writing down what they do, so when I asked for recipes, I often got something along the lines of "well, first you make your roux, add your seasonings, add your meats, add your seafood, and then chopped parsley at the end." I dare anyone to follow this recipe or even to try to figure out what you would be making. The only thing you can be pretty sure of is that you would serve it with rice. I had to ask and ask and ask again: What? When? How much? Chopped or sliced? The most common answer to these questions was "add what you like and just make it like you like to make it." My solution was to constantly ask for clarifications and, whenever possible, watch as each dish was made so that I could write down a recipe that was detailed and descriptive enough for anyone to follow.

Another challenge was figuring out amounts. One person's tablespoon came out of a measuring spoon that had been carefully leveled with the back of a knife while another person's tablespoon actually turned out to be a ladle. All of the recipes in this book were tested at least once in my kitchen, and the amounts you see here adhere to the American measuring cup standard so that you can make something that resembles the actual dish.

Amounts had to be adjusted for another reason as well. Many home cooks' standard recipes will serve thirty or forty people. I have kept some of the original amounts just to give you an idea of the scale of cooking that many of these people do. In other cases, I have reduced the amounts to serve *only* eight or sixteen. To reduce the amounts further, so as to fit the standard American family of four, would give you the wrong idea. New Orleans home cooking is big cooking. Even home cooks who live alone and mainly cook for themselves cannot prepare a pot of food for fewer than ten people. You bet they cried when they rolled their refrigerators and freezers to the curb after Katrina!

Gathering these recipes, I began thinking about how recipes come to us. One woman told me how her cherished family recipes actually all came from "the help" that had been working for her family for generations. Others told me stories about family members or friends who would leave out ingredients on purpose when sharing their recipes, or refuse to share recipes at all—sometimes out of pride, because years and years of fixing something entitles one to secrets and fame, sometimes because they did not approve of the person who asked for the recipe, sometimes because they had themselves received the recipe from someone who had asked them not to share it or because the recipe was considered a family treasure and something that might make or break that family restaurant if it ever became reality. Even when shared, recipes are far from absolute. Two people can use the same recipe and make different things, since everybody cooks based on personal experience. There are both basic and subtle techniques that rarely get spelled out. Still, they make all the difference.

This book aims to be documentary in scope. I wanted to write it because I find what regular people do every day to be both interesting and incredibly important. Places and cultures should be defined by what happens there on a daily basis, because it's the things we do every day that become our lives. Almost every cook in this book considers the cooking he or she does as nothing special, "just ordinary cooking. Just ordinary food." But ordinary cooking and ordinary life in New Orleans seem truly extraordinary when compared to many places in the U.S. where home cooking has become more and more reduced to special occasion cooking for holidays and family affairs.

So, "take what you like, and add what you like," as Aida in Broadmoor says about food, recipes, and life. I hope that is how you will read this book. Listen to the stories. Taste the foods. Enjoy!

You Are Where You Eat

Old School

"My mother taught us how to love and treat people. We were taught that."

MAYOLA BRUMFIELD SERVES UP NOTHIN' BUT LOVE: "As far as food lies, God has blessed us. He still blesses us with food. And for cooking, I love to cook. For company to eat, I love that. And then I always used to keep plenty company.

"Sunday morning, I know somebody's coming. I know that for sure. I'll get up and cook. I'll cook about six different meals, sometimes five. They'll call me, and I'll tell them what I'm cooking and they'll come over. Some Sunday mornings I might stew hen. I might cook some red beans and rice. I might make a potato salad. I might cook some steaks or sometimes I cook greens or cabbage. I'll fix some pork and beans, smoked sausage, whatever they like. And not only Sunday, I'll do during the week, I'll do likewise, because I keep a freezer full of food and I want to cook it. I love to cook. I enjoy cooking. I might come home right now and fix a big pot of gumbo and fry some chicken and stew a hen, because that's what I like. And I love people and I want them to be happy like me. That's joy. On the spur of the moment I might get up and just start cooking because I love to cook. And I love to eat too.

"I loved my neighbors, I miss my neighbors; I had nice neighbors. Sometimes they would buy food for me to cook. They would buy the whole layout. They'd ask me, 'Would you smother this rabbit for me?' I'd say, 'Yes.'

Mayola Ann Brumfield

BORN
1946 in New Orleans, Louisiana

NEIGHBORHOOD
B. W. Cooper

OCCUPATION
Homemaker

HOLY TRINITY
Onion, parsley, garlic powder

GUILTY PLEASURE?
Pie!

And I'd cook it just like I'm stewing a chicken, or sometime I'm putting it in the oven. Some would ask me to cook some greens. Different things. And I would enjoy doing that. I'm happy. And the kids, I would have school kids, my children's friends, they would come even if my kids wasn't there. All come to eat. They still come. They might not come all at one time, but they'll come during the day. Saturday I had my daughters, my grandchildren, I had Yolanda, I had my sister-in-law, I had her son, her two grandchildren, I had a friend of ours, Mr. Lewis, I must have had about twenty-five over here. That was Saturday. That was joy.

"Red beans, they love my beans. And my gumbo. My beans and gumbo. What I put in my gumbo? I would put my smoked sausage, my hot sausage, my gizzards, my stew meat and all that together, and then later on I would put my necks because it don't take long for necks to cook. I slip my crab and shrimps in there and let it cook for a few minutes. Then put my filé, and that's it. I make me a roux, nice and brown, and put in there. I take my time and cut my seasonings real small because the kids really don't like the seasonings, but I cut it so fine they would hardly taste it.

"I was born and raised right on Second and Roman. In my household, it was all the same. My grandmother cooked, my mother cooked, and we had plenty people there to eat all the time. I think the whole block was our family. The whole block. It was so much love for everything. Just beautiful, wonderful. I had a good father, I had a good mother. We ate this, we ate that. My friends would say, 'We ate some of this,' and I said, 'My mama cooked that yesterday too.' They'd say, 'Where do you think we eat at?' Even the teachers, 'Tell Mama to send me a plate.' That's the type of person my mother was. She didn't have no pick and choose. Everybody was welcome. I'm used to everyone being like one big happy family, and I thought every-body lived like that. I thought everybody lived like we lived, but they don't. That's why it hurts sometimes. I was a grown woman, married, when I realized people didn't live like that. But if you've got love in your heart, you're still loving.

"At Calliope [housing project], we had the whole section; we were close to each other. The holidays, they would ask me, show them how to cook their turkeys and hams, and how to make their gumbo. I even gave a supper once or twice. My baby was coming out of school and I needed three hundred dollars. You heard me. I was getting my social security, but the ring ceremony was coming up. I said, 'My baby need her ring. Let me give a supper.' They said, 'What are you going to have?' I said, 'I'm going to have fried chicken, baked macaroni, lettuce and tomato salad, green peas, bread, and cake.' Then I said I was going to have red beans, fried chicken, potato salad, and cake. And I had fish, potato salad, lettuce and tomato, and then I had yakameat. And please believe me, I only wanted three hundred. I said, 'Lord, let me make three hundred. That's all I want, to get that ring.' People don't believe this, but I made almost a thousand dollars. The whole neighborhood came, even the schools. In my own kitchen, in my house, in my project. So I know, with the help of God, that I can do that.

"My husband used to cook too. He cooked everything. He cooked coons, any kind of wild thing, he cooked it. But I didn't like the wild stuff; I am scared of it. I look at it, and scared. He loved to fish, you know the garfish, he would fry that and he would have so much seasonings, that was the best eating you ever had.

"You know what he would do? He would put it up; we had a nail in my house, in the wall, in the cabinet. My cabinets were thicker then. And he would hang the fish there after he cleaned it, and he would tenderloin it like steaks. The fish would be this

big [spreading her arms]. He would hang it up by the mouth. He had a hook. And baby, I had a sharp knife. I never saw nobody else do fish like that.

"My husband brought everything home. He would bring boxes of fruits and things. Sometimes he would bring three, four, five watermelons home, and I always had someone to give it to. It was too much for me, but I had the type of husband who could cook. All kinds. He would take skin and make hog cracklings. Pigskin. Oh, yeah. Taste like the store! I would have pans of cracklings, and I would love it. He would just fry it until it get like that. Sometime he would make corn bread from scratch

On a regular day, Mayola prepares a large pot of red beans and rice with pigs' feet, fried chicken, and corn bread. She welcomes anybody who comes to her door to eat. From left to right: Keishel Williams; Mayola, Clynesha, and Lisa Brumfield; Roy Brown.

and he would put the crackling in it. Yes! It wasn't no Jiffy. My husband made corn bread from scratch!

"My whole family love to cook. We all cook and love to cook. And it'd be good."

—*As told by Mayola Brumfield*

Codfish Balls

Mayola says, "I never see anyone cook this now. You talk about a different time."

Serves 6

2 cans fish flakes or 1 pound finely flaked cooked white
    fish
2 eggs
2 cups mashed potatoes (with 2 tablespoons butter) not
    too tightly packed
2 heaping tablespoons each of minced onion, celery,
    green bell pepper, green onion, and parsley
Tony Chachere's Creole Seasoning to taste (about 1 tea-
    spoon) or salt and pepper
½ cup flour
½ stick butter for frying

Mix fish, egg, potato, and all fresh and dry seasonings together. Form large meatballs. Put flour on a plate. Roll each meatball in flour, pat until flat and about half an inch thick. Fry codfish balls (cakes, really) in butter over medium fire until golden. Serve with rice or as a sandwich on French bread with lettuce and tomatoes.

Meat Loaf with Hard-boiled Eggs

"Every slice is a piece of egg you can eat, but you can do it with shrimps too, the same way," instead of hard-boiled eggs.

Serves 8

2 pounds ground beef
1 green bell pepper, finely chopped
1 rib celery, finely chopped
2 yellow onions, finely chopped
2 cloves garlic, finely chopped
5 sprigs of parsley, chopped
½ cup breadcrumbs
Salt and pepper
2 raw eggs + 4 hard-boiled and peeled
2 cans cream of mushroom soup

Mix all ingredients except for hard-boiled eggs and soup. Press about half the mixture into a greased meat loaf pan. Line the hard-boiled eggs up the middle. Add the other half of the meat mixture, covering eggs, and bake in the oven at 350 degrees for 40 minutes or until the top is brown. Transfer meat loaf to a small casserole dish. Top with cream of mushroom soup and put meat loaf back in the oven for 15 minutes.

Yakamein

Mayola Brumfield learned to cook yakamein from her mother, Mayola Brown, who was born in 1924 and has more than one hundred grandchildren, great-grandchildren, and great-great-grandchildren. "My mama made yakameat. I'm going to make some today. If you don't like it you don't like it, but I love it. All my family make yakameat. They makes it good. I've seen people make it with pork chops, roast, any kind of meat. It doesn't make a difference." If you are sensitive to monosodium glutamate (MSG), you can skip the Accent and add an extra teaspoon of Tony's.

Serves 16

4 pounds boneless stew meat
1 teaspoon Accent
1 teaspoon McCormick's Season-All
1 teaspoon Tony Chachere's Creole Seasoning
1 teaspoon onion powder
4 beef bouillon cubes

4 tablespoons vegetable oil
2 pounds spaghetti
16 eggs, hard-boiled and peeled
2 bunches green onions, chopped
Soy sauce
Hot sauce
Ketchup

Boil meat, covered, until it almost falls apart (about 2 hours) in 5 quarts of water with seasonings and oil. Take out meat and pull it apart, adding it back to the pot. Cook spaghetti separately.

Serve yakamein as follows: Put some spaghetti in the bottom of your bowl. Then add green onions and one hard-boiled egg, either whole or in pieces. Top with meat and a little more than 1 cup of the cooking liquid. Season to taste with soy sauce, hot sauce, and ketchup.

Where Y'at, Yakamein?

Yakamein is somewhat of a mystery dish. Some people believe that it was American GIs coming back from Korea in the 1950s who brought the recipe for yakamein with them. Who knows, but it is an interesting black New Orleans take on Asian noodle soup. Yakamein was never really served in restaurants. Big bowls of steamy beef broth with spaghetti, hard-boiled egg, hot sauce, soy sauce, and ketchup usually come out the back of a bar, late at night. Yakamein is also dished out at corner stores, as well as from stands and vans along parade routes. The dish has become less visible in later years, but is still prepared and enjoyed at home by many black New Orleans families on a budget.

The Irish Is in the Beholder

"Which came first, the beer or the bread?"

William Joseph Noel Chabanel Patrick Murphy

BORN
1943 in New Orleans, Louisiana

NEIGHBORHOOD
Irish Channel

OCCUPATION
Museum curator

HOLY TRINITY
Mayo, mustard, ketchup

COFFEE TRICK?
Cinnamon and eggshell on the coffee grounds for flavor and less bitterness

BILL MURPHY TELLS HOW IRISH FOOD CAN COME FROM ANYWHERE— EVEN A KEG: "The Irish Channel was a rough neighborhood for a very long time, and it was an Irish neighborhood, primarily. Later, a lot of the grocery store owners and butchers were actually Italians. The Irish were very fond of spaghetti, and they sort of took that over from their Italian neighbors. The Irish were very fond of German potato salad too. That's the only kind of potato salad my mother ever made. You don't eat it warm, if you're Irish. You eat it cold, with a lot of mayonnaise.

"I am half German, by the way, so I have that mixture of Irish food and German food in my background. Both my grandmothers were German— Barbara Becker and Barbara Sieger—so we always had this mix. And it shows when you physically see me, because I'm not a small person. I've been well fed my entire life.

"A lot of people fail to realize, they often associate corned beef and cabbage with the Irish, but corned beef and cabbage is actually a Jewish dish. The Irish coming into this country, up around New York, learned how to eat corned beef and cabbage, because cabbage was probably the cheapest vegetable and corned beef was probably the cheapest kind of meat that you could buy. And the Irish, like they do a lot of times, they threw a couple of Irish potatoes in the pot. Because the Irish are very fond of potatoes, you have to understand.

"For parties, one of our favorite things was hot dogs and chili. And beer. And if someone made chili, they would put chili powder in it. But the same recipe that was used for the chili was also used for making Italian meat sauce. Italian meat sauce was simply the chili without the chili powder in it. Sometimes you would look in your refrigerator and you would have meat sauce, and it'd have a plus or a minus. The plus was for hot dogs and the minus was for an Italian dinner.

"New Orleans is a mishmash, a mix of cultures. And that also includes the culinary part of it, in what people ate. People adopted each other's menus, each other's food habits. You know, there is a lot of African American cooking that's made its way into the Irish cooking. My mother made a dynamite gumbo, a seafood gumbo. And basically what it was was an okra stew with shrimp and crabs in it. Also fried plantains. She made a batter out of egg yolk. After she dipped it in the egg yolk, she dipped it in granulated sugar and she fried it. And then you ate that with sugarcane molasses on top of it.

"The Irish didn't have a lot of sweets. There was no real tradition of eating sweets in Ireland; it's only when the Irish started to come to the United States. In my family, they were really into candy. My sister used to make fudge. Her fudge was basically sugar that she hardened in a pan, put a little condensed milk in it, and a little bit of chocolate. She used five pounds of sugar. You'd bite into it and it had a crystalline structure. You could grind it up again and use it as a sweetener in your coffee. Two pieces of that fudge sucked all the moisture out of your mouth.

"Sweets are a reward in Irish families. In some families, Italian families, they cook with sugar, like two tablespoons in spaghetti sauce. The Irish use sweets as a reward in raising their children.

If I got a good report card, I got a nickel a day to spend at school. And for a nickel a day, I could buy three boxes of licorice snaps, or ten licorice whips. If you didn't get a good report card, you didn't get a nickel and you went into sugar withdrawal until your next report card. At two thirty in the afternoon there would be a line in front of Ms. Morrison's sweetshop.

"When the potato blight hit Ireland, people don't really have a comprehension for how quickly it spread. People went to bed and the potatoes were fine in the field. In the morning, when the sun came up, the potatoes would be spongy and rotten. And because they were dependent on that food alone, I think when they came to the United States they had this option of all of these different types of food, and they took some from here and some from there and some from somewhere else, and they made it their own. You have Italian cuisine and you have French cuisine, but there is no particularly Irish American cuisine.

"In the Irish Channel, beer was definitely considered a food. My father was a temperance individual, we never had an open bottle of liquor in the house. But beer went with everything in the Irish Channel. Red beans and rice, hot dogs and chili, meatballs and spaghetti. You always had to have beer; beer was always there.

"Also, people in this neighborhood were very much into bread. There were three bakeries. When you went to Elzie's in the afternoon to get the groceries for Mom, you were sent down a little further down the street to get a loaf of French bread. French bread was one of the things I was raised on as a tradition. Sometimes, instead of eating dessert after a meal, you drank a cup of coffee and ate your French bread and butter, which is another reason I'm the size that I am.

"You know what one of my favorite sandwiches is? Fried

Almost the whole family comes to Bill's and his sister Bernadette's house on Magazine Street on St. Patrick's Day to enjoy food, drink, and the parade passing by. James Murphy, Barbara Rizzo, and Bill Murphy enjoy a good laugh when they're too full to eat anymore.

Spam with a slice of orange American cheese. You put it on toast and you put the Spam while the Spam is still hot, and the cheese melts. Good sandwich. A lot of people in my family, especially those who fought in the Second World War, wouldn't eat Spam. You know what Spam stands for? Specially Packaged American Meat. My sister used to like it paneed. She would put it in a batter, like a paneed pork chop. Paneed meat, *und ein Bier*."

—*As told by Bill Murphy*

Liver Po-Boy with Smothered Onions

"The best po-boy sandwich in the world is a liver sandwich on French bread with smothered onions. You butter the bread on the inside and you get a little dish of liver gravy, so you can dip. My doctor only allows me to eat that once a year. Liver, lots of people don't like it, but it was one of the big sellers here."

Serves 2

1 pound liver
1 cup milk
1 cup flour
1 teaspoon salt
1 teaspoon black pepper
4 tablespoons oil, lard, or bacon grease
2 yellow onions, thinly sliced
1 cup water
1 loaf French bread
Butter

Slice liver and soak in milk for a couple of hours in the refrigerator. Mix flour, salt, and black pepper together in a bowl. Remove liver from milk and dredge in seasoned flour. Panfry on both sides in fat over medium heat until liver is crisp and cooked through. Remove and drain on newspaper or paper towels. Fry onion in remaining fat. Add 1–2 tablespoons of the seasoned flour to make a roux. Add water and simmer to thicken. Dress bread with butter and liver. Scoop up some of the onion pieces and put them over the liver. Pour remaining gravy into a small, shallow dish. Dip and eat.

Enough Beer to Flood the City

In the years just after Prohibition, New Orleans had as many as eight big brewing companies all started or run by Germans or German descendants: Jackson Brewing Company, with the Fabacher family, made Jax Beer; Standard Brewing Company, with brewmaster Waffenschmidt, made Wirthbru Beer and Rex; New Orleans Brewing Company, with manager Gronstedt, made Four X, Eagle, and Old Union Beer; Dixie Brewing Company, started by Merz, made Dixie Beer; American Brewing Company, with Schlieder and then Schmedtje (along with Sullivan, who probably was Irish) made Regal Beer. Finally, National Brewing Company made Eagle Beer and Double Eagle Ale, while Union Brewing Company made Old Union Beer. Falstaff Brewing Company, which started in St. Louis, Missouri, bought out National Brewing Company in 1936 and started to make, with brewer Krafft, Falstaff Beer in New Orleans. All these breweries were already operating before—and survived—Prohibition.

The Mayor of Poland Avenue

"I'm only going to give you a suggestion if you want."

JOANNE CIEUTAT FOLLOWS HER MOTHER'S RECIPES IN THE HOUSE HER GRANDFATHER BUILT: "I cook every day, but I'm not a baker. You're either really good at cooking dinners, or you're either good at baking. And I do no baking at all. I cook.

"I cook for Ms. Josie, and then two days a week I go home and cook for my family. Ms. Josie has to have special meals because she's diabetic. So she eats very good gourmet meals even though they're salt free, low fat, and no sugar. And I've been with her nine years. Even on the two days that I'm not here I cook, like today I'm cooking for tomorrow, the two meals for tomorrow. But I love it; I really do like cooking. Italian, like Ms. Josie. In fact, my grandmother came from the same part of Italy that her grandmother was from, so she likes my cooking. My mother's mother came here to marry my grandpa; it was one of those match marriages. Sicilians married Sicilians. She was eighteen.

"Do you want me to give you an example of what I cook today? For lunch she had liver and grits. She loves calf liver, sliced really thin. Tonight she'll have barbecued chicken, a leg and a thigh, some smothered cabbage with onions, and potato salad. And for tomorrow, I've cooked a roast for her with potatoes and mushrooms and carrots for supper, string beans on the side, and

Camille Joanne Cieutat

BORN
1937 in New Orleans, Louisiana

NEIGHBORHOOD
Bywater

OCCUPATION
Caregiver

HOLY TRINITY
Olive oil, onion, garlic

CHEESE ON SEAFOOD?
Not in Italy—but most definitely in New Orleans!

for lunch she's going to have stuffed peppers. So I guess you'd say I cook! Fourteen hot meals for Ms. Josie every week. I don't repeat anything within a month for her. Breakfast is the same every day: oatmeal, prunes, piece of toast, and a cup of coffee. She eats really healthy. I'm not bragging.

"My brothers, we all live next door to one another. We're still in the same house that my mother grew up in on Poland Avenue. It's three doubles in a row. I live in one; my brother lives in the other half. My niece used to live in one, but my

Joanne does her shopping at Dorignac's at seven in the morning when she's practically alone in the store, except for the employees. "Hey, Ms. Joanne! What are you cooking today?"

brother has moved back. My other brother has moved back. My son lives with me. It's nice living next to your family because when you cook a lot you can share. You can't make a little pot of soup.

"My mother never let me cook with her in the kitchen. I was the dishwasher. I cleaned up. When my mother was dying, she was sick in the bed with cancer for nineteen months. I guess that's the way God let me learn how to cook, because she was bedridden and my brothers hooked up walkie-talkies for us, you can talk back and forth. I'd be in the kitchen and she'd be in her hospital bed and she wanted me to cook so all my brothers and their family would come over to eat. That's one thing about Italians. If you cook they come to see you. If you don't cook they don't go see you. They love to eat. I have four brothers; I'm the only girl. So she would teach me from the bed. Do this, do that. And that was a lot of her recipes there. After she died, I stayed in the family home and continued cooking for my brothers.

"I make Milanese gravy just like my mama did. That's my mother's recipe and my grandmother's. Milanese is for St. Joseph. I make a huge pot because they all love it, and you make it from tomato sauce, tomato puree, fresh fennel, sardines, capers, pine nuts, currants. It's got sardines plus anchovies. Then you serve that over a number seven pasta.

"I do my mother's stuffed cabbage, which is a big project. You make your stuffing out of pork, veal, and beef, the three ground meats, and onions and garlic and Italian cheese, and a little bit breadcrumbs. Then you parboil the whole cabbage. While it's hot, you open the cabbage like a rose. You start stuffing it from the center and when you're finished it looks like the cabbage you started with, except it's twice as big. And you bake it for about one hour, covered with some olive oil and foil, tight, in the oven. Then you slice it like you would cake. It's very good, but that's once a year. Nobody knows how to do anything simple.

"I have two granddaughters. One's an attorney and the other one is getting her Ph.D. at Vanderbilt. They don't cook. No indeed. I don't know what they'll ever do when they get married. I don't know what's going to happen to those girls."

—As told by Joanne Cieutat

New Orleans Food Seasons

Joanne's maternal grandparents had a produce stand in the French Market, while her paternal grandparents were farmers in St. Bernard. Joanne is a stickler for fresh ingredients. She cooks according to New Orleans's four seasons: crawfish (roughly spring), crab (all year, but most popular in summer), shrimp (brown shrimp in spring and summer, white shrimp in fall), and oysters (all year, but most popular in fall and winter). She also buys local fruit and vegetables when they become ripe and plentiful.

Spring brings beets, turnips, carrots, cauliflower, green peas, green onions, radishes, spinach, strawberries, blueberries, and blackberries.

Summer brings figs, muscadine grapes, peaches, plums, watermelons, cantaloupes, snap beans, lima beans, okra, peppers, cucumber, squash, tomatoes, eggplants, and onions.

Fall brings navel oranges, persimmons, pecans, pumpkins, sweet potatoes, turnips, garlic, and more peppers.

Winter brings lemons, satsumas, early strawberries, beets, broccoli, cabbage, greens, and mirlitons.

Cucuzza with Shrimp

"Cucuzza is a long-neck squash. Light green, long and skinny. The color of a mirliton, that color green. People would grow them in their backyards and give them to you for free. Everybody had a cucuzza vine, as everybody had a mirliton vine in New Orleans. I call it Italian squash, me."

Serves 6

1 cucuzza
1 teaspoon salt
1 yellow onion, finely chopped
4 cloves garlic, finely chopped
2 tablespoons olive oil
1 (14½-ounce) can Del Monte Petite Cut Tomatoes
   (Zesty Jalapeños)
1 pound peeled large shrimp
¼ cup olive oil
½ cup grated Romano cheese
Salt
Pepper

Peel cucuzza with potato peeler and cut in half lengthwise. If seeds are very big, remove some with a spoon. Cut cucuzza into ½-inch-thick slices. Cover with cold water in a big pot, add salt, and simmer for 10–15 minutes until tender but not mushy. Strain, reserving some of the water. In the same pot, sauté onion and garlic in olive oil. Add tomatoes. Simmer, covered, over low-to-medium heat for 20 minutes. Wash and drain shrimp. Add shrimp and cucuzza, cover and simmer for another 10 minutes. Turn off heat. Consistency should be like stew; if

dry, add about 1 cup cucuzza water. Add olive oil and Romano cheese. Add salt and pepper to taste. Serve over pasta or rice.

Vegetable Soup

Vegetarians beware! "I call it vegetable soup. You would probably call it beef stew, because I put roast in it to make it. I'm in the habit of saying vegetable soup because it's all vegetables with the meat, and my mother called it vegetable soup."

Serves 12

1 large osso buco bone
2 pounds boneless chuck roast, cut into big chunks
1 (14½-ounce) can Del Monte Petite Cut Tomatoes
   (Zesty Jalapeños)
2 quarts water
1 can Swanson's Chicken Broth
½ teaspoon tarragon
1 good shake Emeril's Italian Essence
1 large yellow onion, quartered
1 large turnip, peeled and cut into chunks
1 pound fresh green beans, ends cut
3 carrots, peeled and sliced
3 ribs celery, in pieces
3 red potatoes, skin on, cut into chunks
½ small head cabbage, coarsely chopped
Salt and black pepper
¼ bunch fresh parsley, coarsely chopped
1 nest angel hair pasta

Cook first 8 ingredients (ending with onion) covered over low heat for almost 2 hours until meat is very tender. Take bone out, adding meat (if any left on bone) back to pot. Also, break up meat into smaller pieces. Add turnip and simmer for 10 minutes. Add green beans and simmer for another 10 minutes. Add carrots, celery, potatoes, and cabbage. Simmer for 10 minutes more. Add salt and pepper to taste. Turn heat off, adding parsley and angel hair pasta. Cover and wait 10 minutes before serving.

Heads and Tails Crawfish Bisque

Joanne starts making this on Holy Thursday and serves it to her extended family on Good Friday every year. She prepares the stuffing the first day and lets it sit overnight in the refrigerator. "You don't leave the kitchen when you make this." This is an Italian-style version with a strong tomato flavor, without roux and not pureed. If your stomach is sensitive to tomatoes, you can replace some or most of the tomato sauce in this recipe with the same amount seafood stock thickened with roux, holding back on the sugar.

Stuffing for heads:
1 green bell pepper, finely chopped
2 pounds yellow onions, finely chopped
2 heads garlic, finely chopped
3 bay leaves
¼ cup olive oil
1 stale po-boy loaf

4 pounds crawfish tails, chopped
1 tablespoon Emeril's Italian Essence
1 tablespoon Tony Chachere's Creole Seasoning
Salt and pepper to taste
Italian breadcrumbs (if needed)

To prepare heads:
200–250 cleaned crawfish heads
1 tablespoon baking soda

For bisque:
3 (29-ounce) cans Hunt's diced tomatoes
3 (29-ounce) cans Hunt's tomato sauce
2 (10-ounce) cans diced Rotel tomatoes
1 green bell pepper, finely chopped
2 pounds yellow onions, finely chopped
2 heads garlic, finely chopped
3 bay leaves
1 cup sugar
1 tablespoon Emeril's Italian Essence
Kitchen Bouquet (for color)
2 cups white wine
1 pound Louisiana crawfish tails, whole
Salt, pepper, and Tony Chachere's Creole Seasoning

Holy Thursday: Make stuffing for heads by sautéing bell peppers, yellow onions, and garlic in olive oil. Add bay leaves and cook over low heat in a covered pan for 30 minutes, stirring from time to time. Break bread into pieces and soak in water. After a few minutes, strain bread in colander, pressing out water. Add bread to seasonings and sauté for 10 minutes. Add chopped crawfish tails, Emeril's, and Tony's. Add salt and pepper to taste. Add breadcrumbs, if necessary, until you get the right consistency (stuffing forms soft balls). Cover and let cool. Refrigerate overnight.

Good Friday: Prepare already-cleaned heads by boiling them in a big stockpot of water with baking soda for a few minutes. Rinse well, discard water, and let heads dry. In same stockpot, add all cans of tomato, rinsing them out with a minimum of water. Add bell pepper, onion, and garlic. Add bay leaves, sugar, Emeril's, and Kitchen Bouquet until the bisque becomes terra-cotta red. Bring to a boil and simmer, covered, for 2 hours. In the meantime, stuff shells. Place stuffed shells on cookie sheets and lightly brown them in the oven at 375 degrees for 10–15 minutes. Add wine and whole crawfish tails to bisque. Add salt, pepper, and Tony's to taste. Simmer for a few minutes. Add heads, turning carefully. Bring bisque to a boil, turn off heat, cover, and let rest on the stove for about 4 hours. Reheat before serving. Serve with rice, French bread, and a side salad.

Hunting for Turtle Gumbo

"I had to tell some girlfriends, 'You can keep what you've got, because I'm going hunting Saturday morning.'"

NUMA MARTINEZ REMEMBERS PULLING HIS DINNER FROM THE SWAMPS:
"This is my humble abode. I'm an old man. Just had a birthday. Went to church, went to the casino. Lost my ass off.

"I'm not pure Spanish. I've got Choctaw, I've got black, I've got French, I've got Spanish. I've got four of them buggers running through me. In the state of Louisiana, if you're one-sixteenth black you're considered black. Do I look black [laughs]?

"My old man taught us all that we knew about hunting. I miss him. He didn't like you to waste a shot at a duck. He didn't like you to shoot at a rabbit and miss a rabbit. 'What's wrong with you, boy? You missed that duck? Waste no bullet. Bullets are expensive.'

"In the springtime, Daddy used to take me back out there in Chalmette, hunting cowan turtles to make cowan gumbo, or we'd be lucky enough to catch them coming across the highway after big rain. When you want to kill a snapping turtle, cowan turtle, you get him to put his mouth locked down on a broomstick. Don't fool with the head! Leave the head alone. When he

Numa James Martinez

BORN
1945 in New Orleans, Louisiana

NEIGHBORHOOD
Sixth and Seventh Wards

OCCUPATION
Retired school principal

HOLY TRINITY
Water, salt, pepper

HURRICANE PREPAREDNESS?
One electric stove, one gas stove!

got his jaw locked on that broomstick, you pull that head out. It might take two people to do it but I've seen my daddy do it just by himself. You put this foot on the tail, bring that neck out and take the hatchet, cut the head off. One swell, swift swoop. Then you hang him on the fence for two hours, let him bleed out. Bleed, bleed, bleed, bleed. You can hang him with a coat hanger on a chain-link fence. Once he stop drip-drip, turn that shell on the side. My daddy had a shingle hatchet that the roofers use, it's very sharp, you can shave with it, a couple of whacks, get the shell off. Like cracking an egg open. Then you've got all the meat looking at you.

"My mama had the gumbo pot. You got the spices, the herbs, vegetables, potatoes. Don't go in the kitchen when them old grandmas are in there cooking! Oh, no. Go take your bath, go cut your grass, go change your oil, go to the movies. Don't go in the kitchen. Taboo! The kitchen is for the women. Boom! Men stay out of the kitchen. Once that gumbo is finished and you've got your potato salad, your sweet potatoes, your French bread, your root beer, the lady of the house will call one time, 'Gumbo ready!' And if your ass ain't in the house, you don't eat. So, you mingle around the house, you swap lies about the rabbit hunting and the deer hunting and the duck hunting and the *poule d'eau* shooting.

"My daddy was a market hunter. To supplement the income, my dad used to go hunting ducks by the Bonnet Carré Spillway and sell the ducks to Antoine's and the Court of Two Sisters two dollars a pair. And if he had a good day, he would come back with eight, maybe ten pair of ducks. Walked from the Bonnet Carré Spillway to catch the streetcar at Carrollton and Claiborne. Catch that streetcar and come down St. Charles Avenue. Nobody mess with him, with them twenty ducks around his waist and the double-barreled shotgun. That's the way it was back then. Get off, go to the back door of the kitchen. 'Hey, Martinez, how many you've got, *cher*?' Twenty dollars like two thousand dollars back then. You have to remember, that time span, that window. Like my daddy say, if you're not going to eat it, don't shoot it. But if you want to eat that duck, shoot that son of a bitch and don't miss!

"A lot of people came back after Katrina and didn't have a place to stay. 'My house is yours.' Germaine Mack, she's an excellent cook, she stayed here with me for about six months. 'What you feel like eating, Nunu?' 'I feel like eating one of them big old steaks.' So big mama Germaine Mack would get in the kitchen. She'd tell the other little old ladies, 'Get the hell out the way, this is my kitchen.' There always have to have one big mama in the kitchen that was over everything in the kitchen. She would bring me a tray. Porterhouse steak, string beans, asparagus, creamed potatoes, green peas, cranberry, corn bread, half of a po-boy loaf, and a Barq's root beer. 'That 'a hold you, huh?' I said, 'In about an hour, I'll be hungry again.' 'Say what?!' 'Yeah, where the dessert?' 'What you got, a hole in your foot?' About half an hour, forty-five minutes later she would come in with about eight scoops of Napoleon ice cream, the three flavors, and a big jar of chocolate syrup. Said, 'Goddamn! For a little skinny son of a bitch, you put some food down!' I said, 'I'm hungry, Mama.'

"She would do little knickknacks like apple pie. Oh Lord, apple pie, cherry pie, and pecan pie. I have one tree in the backyard that makes the big, big pecans and one tree that makes them teeny-weeny small pecans. My cousin Albert and his wife, Mildred, and big mama Germaine, they come get the pecans and make pecan pralines and pecan pie. Oh Lord. Child! Mil, boy, she's a big mama, be about the same as Germaine Mack. The best cooks are the big mamas. Ain't no skinny people like

"This one ought to feed about thirty people," Numa says, happy to once again hold a snapping turtle by the tail.

us. Big mamas! Mildred make you holler for a dollar when she make 'em pecan pralines.

"A neighborhood is one square block, four corners. It got so good around here, it got so good that when we went on a rabbit hunt, oh child. Them grandmas were up before the crack of dawn, going in them kitchens and getting them old cast-iron pots out. You could hear them, clink, clink, clink. Yes, ma'am. What Mama used to do, if we killed too many rabbits, 'Numa, after you finish cleaning the boat, take a pair of rabbits to Ms. Evelyn's house, take a pair of rabbits over there to Ms. Imelda's house, take a pair of rabbits over there to Lorraine's house, take a pair of rabbits to Sadie's house.' Sometime we came back with sixty-eight rabbits, sometime eighty-two. Everybody in the neighborhood would watch out for each other, neighbor watch

out for neighbor. Them old grandmas would say, 'Young man, don't you go over there by Mr. Martinez and take nothing out that man's yard. I owe him. You go fool with Mr. Martinez, we can't get any more rabbits, I'm going to bust your behind. Mr. Martinez gave us a pair of rabbits that you ate last week!' That's how everybody got, even the Italians. Mr. Joe said, 'Nunu!' *Ei, paesano, come va?*' 'Come get this pasta for your mama.' 'But Mr. Joe, my mama ain't Italian.' 'Boy! Come get this pasta with the rabbits!' 'Yes, sir!' 'Mama, Mr. Joe sent pasta with rabbit meat.' 'Oh, ain't that nice. Tell Mr. Joe thank you.' 'Mr. Joe, my mama said *grazie*.' 'Boy, how did you learn to speak Italian?' 'I listened to you, Mr. Joe.'"

—*As told by Numa Martinez*

Fish and Shrimp Sauce Piquante

This recipe comes from Numa's favorite nephew, Herman "Junny Boy" Broussard, who lives in New Iberia. His version contains no fat, but he won't get mad if you decide to add some.

Serves 10

2 large cans tomato sauce

1 small can tomato paste

2 yellow onions, minced

Hot or sweet peppers (cayenne, Mexican chili, hot banana, sweet banana, bell, or jalapeño), diced

2–3 ribs celery, chopped

2 tablespoons minced garlic

2 pounds redfish or catfish, in chunks

1½ pounds peeled large shrimp

1–2 teaspoons Season-All

½ cup chopped green onion tops

½ bunch fresh parsley, chopped

Simmer tomato sauce and tomato paste in a large pot, covered, for 1½ hours, stirring often. Add yellow onion, peppers, celery, and garlic. Cover and continue to simmer for 1 hour. Season fish and shrimp with Season-All and then add to sauce. Add green onion tops and parsley. Simmer for another 15 minutes. Serve over Louisiana long-grain rice.

Hot Sauce

Hot things come to those who wait! This recipe is also from Herman "Junny Boy" Broussard.

70% fresh Tabasco peppers

30% fresh habañero peppers

Distilled white vinegar

Salt

Remove stems and heads from peppers. Pack tightly into a gallon jug. Pour in vinegar about halfway up. Pour in about 1½ cups salt. Top off with vinegar. Seal airtight. Keep jug in room temperature in a dark area (bottom cabinet or closet) for at

The Corner Store Gourmet

Cooking for one is particularly difficult for New Orleanians who are used to cooking large. Did you ever hear of a gumbo or jambalaya recipe for one? Even four? Probably not, if you live in Louisiana. Local bachelors, widows and widowers, migrant workers without families, and other singles continue to rely on the kindness of neighbors and the neighborhood grocery store for daily sustenance. The corner store is always a sure source of canned goods, chips, soda, and beer but also of hard-boiled eggs, pickled pigs' lips, po-boys, and sometimes a Styrofoam clamshell's worth of red beans and rice, turkey necks, fried chicken, fried rice, fried noodles, boiled sausage, ham hocks, and cabbage, usually cheap and surprisingly tasty.

least 2 years, the longer the better. Strain peppers and run them in a blender (fill about halfway up with peppers) with ½ cup fresh vinegar (or enough to thin sauce) per batch. Bottle and enjoy, but be careful! This stuff can burn your eyes out.

Creole Pecan Pralines

Pralines are part of Louisiana's bittersweet history. Sugar fueled the colony, giving rise to large plantations and increasing the demand for slave labor. At the same time, sugar made it possible for some slaves to buy their freedom by selling sweets like pralines. This recipe comes from Numa's cousin Albert's wife, Mildred Martinez. She in turn got it from a friend some fifty years ago. The recipe, including the instructions, is almost the same as Louisiana senator Allen J. Ellender's recipe printed on the back of the Bergeron Shelled Pecans bag. The only difference is Mildred's addition of vanilla. (Author's note: You can easily use fewer nuts than the recipe calls for, but if you add more you might not have enough sugar mixture to hold everything together. Stir and stir and stir before you start spooning out the mixture. The sugar must crystallize, or you'll have a sticky mess.)

2 cups granulated sugar
1 cup dark or light brown sugar
1 stick butter (¼ pound)
1 tablespoon vanilla
1 cup milk
2 tablespoons Karo syrup
4 cups pecan halves or pieces

Put all the ingredients except the pecans in a 3-quart saucepan and cook for about 20 minutes. After boiling starts, stir occasionally. Add the pecans and cook the mixture until the liquid forms a soft ball when a little is dropped into cold water. Stir well and then drop by spoonfuls on waxed paper. Place a few sheets of newspaper beneath the waxed paper. I find it convenient to place a small table near the stove over which I put a few sheets of newspaper, and then put the waxed paper over that.

Una Buena Mujer

"I was a soccer coach for girls in Mexico. I baked cookies for them, cakes. But if they won a game, I made tamales."

BELLAZAR WILCOX FROM MEXICO FINDS FREEDOM IN A TERRYTOWN KITCHEN: "I am from Poza Rica. The taste is Veracruz. Poza Rica is six hours' drive from Veracruz. When I was seven years old, I worked with my daddy in the fields, planting orange trees and bananas and harvesting bananas, oranges, papaya. My dad has an orchard there. Weekends we worked all day from six to five. Every weekend. My brother and my daddy and me.

"Ten years old my mama taught me how to cook. I was thirteen when I left my parents and went to work in a grocery store, earning money to go to high school. I made a deal with my father that I would pay for high school and then my dad would pay for college. He say, 'I don't like it, but okay.' I was making cakes from five in the morning to one in the afternoon, and then I went to school from three in the afternoon to eight at night. I liked the work. I like to work. I worked the cash register, I baked, I cleaned, and I cooked. And then I worked at night. I finished school, I came back at eight o'clock, and I decorated cakes for the next day. I lived in the grocery store. I only saw my parents once a month. It was hard.

"I still make cakes. For friends, or some people call me. I make cakes for them, twenty dollars each. They're Mexican cakes. I make chocolate, vanilla,

Bellazar Wilcox

BORN
1978 in Poza Rica, Mexico

NEIGHBORHOOD
Terrytown

OCCUPATION
Ama de casa (soul of the house)

HOLY TRINITY
Tomato, onion, jalapeño

FAVORITE PEPPER?
Chipotle

strawberry, *tres leches*, that's what I like the most, it's the three milks: condensed milk, evaporated milk, and cream. Rich but good.

"I cook two or three days a week because my husband cooks too, he cooks for me. I make enchiladas, meats, chicken with tomatoes and jalapeño peppers. He cooks barbecue. I like his barbecue. Men don't cook in Mexico, no! My dad, now he cooks some, because he's been coming here for maybe twenty years, he comes and he goes. He works here in order to get plants over there, supplies and what he needs for the orchard. Now he cooks, now he helps me in the kitchen sometimes. But before? Nothing. In Mexico, no! It's a woman's job. It's your job to cook,

Bellazar bakes lavish Mexican cakes, testing the patience of her sister-in-law Adela Cardenas's children, Cristina, Marlen, and Daniel Hernandez.

raise children, clean the house, and you stay in the house. You don't go to the store, nothing. You only work in the house. But not me. I work. My husband is not Mexican.

"I cook lunch for construction workers. My family is in construction. I make lunch for them and the rest of the workers. Chicken, pork, beef, tamales, tacos, different tacos, and pork skins. I prepare everything on plates, the food and the rice and the beans and six tortillas too. I make the tortillas. Not all the workers are Mexican; they're from Honduras, Colombia. The

Hondurans always ask me for yuca and chicharrones, or beef soup with yuca. If the ingredients are over here, then I make it, but I cook Mexican. I make everything Mexican. I make New Orleans food too, but I add a Mexican taste. I always put beans on the side.

"I don't cook like my mother. We use the same ingredients but people say it's different, different seasonings. And my daddy too, he says my food is different. When I used to go visit them, I didn't cook. I didn't cook at my mother's house. I could help, but I let my mother cook. Competition does not help when you want to put the right seasonings into the food, and I want to season the way I want to. Sometimes you feel like free cooking, cooking your best, but you're afraid of the criticism. Sometimes I don't want to give it all.

"If you're a woman in Mexico and you do not cook, people will say you are lazy, that you are not a good woman. Mexican women have to make cooking their interest. If you're a man in Mexico and your woman is not a good cook, you change woman.

Cambia de mujer. When I was sixteen years old I had a boyfriend, he went to my house, he ate my food and he said, 'You're a good girl, you're a good woman.' In Mexico, if you're a woman and you cook good, you're a good woman. If you're a woman and you go to work, you're not necessarily a good woman. But if you don't cook, you're not really a woman.

"I came to New Orleans in 2003. This is the first time I've lived in the U.S. My cooking has changed since I came here but I can't tell you how, just that the taste is different. I'm learning about New Orleans dishes, my husband helps me. Crawfish, barbecue, spaghetti and meatballs. Red beans too. I like my husband's food. Because he likes my food, I like his food too. I think I will stay here for a very long time."

—*As told by Bellazar Wilcox*

The Proof Is in the Pot

Because of racism and limited opportunities for free people of color in Louisiana in the mid-1800s, hundreds of free, black families left and moved to Mexico. Most of them settled in the area between Veracruz, Mexico's largest port city at the time, and Tampico, with regular traffic to and from New Orleans. Their descendants seldom know that their ancestors came from Louisiana. Instead, they think of themselves and many of their family traditions as French. Their cooking, however, is clearly connected to New Orleans. Veracruz Creole families still grow okra, prepare bombo (gumbo), and indulge in crêpes. These foods are not unheard of in other parts of Mexico, but are decidedly more common among people with Louisiana ancestry. According to author Mary Gehman, who is studying the Creole émigrés to Mexico, some families now obtain filé, the powdered sassafras leaves used to thicken gumbo, from connections in California, another haven for New Orleans Creoles looking for a better life. The shipping connection between New Orleans and Mexico might also help explain why hot peppers, which are native to Mexico, became more important in Louisiana cooking than in the rest of the South.

Pork Tamales

Tamales are incredibly versatile. Once you get a hang of the basic idea, you can do pretty much anything you want. Bellazar's tamales are easy to make, and the flavors are straightforward.

Makes 30–40 tamales, serving 15–20

Filling:

20 dried guajillo chilies
1 small yellow onion
1 clove garlic
1 pound fresh tomatoes
1 teaspoon salt
3 pounds pork meat, diced very small

Corn mush:

2.2 pounds (1 kilogram) Maseca instant corn masa mix
¼ pound rich-tasting pork lard (manteca)
¼ cup vegetable oil
1 tablespoon salt (or enough to taste)
8 cups water or more

For assembly:

2 (1-pound) packages fresh or frozen banana leaves or about
   10 large banana leaves without holes or tears from your yard,
   or 1 (6-ounce) package dried cornhusks

Immerse cornhusks (if used) in boiling water, turn off heat, and let soak for about 2 hours. You might need something heavy to weight them down. Rinse cornhusks to remove dirt and loose threads, set aside. If using banana leaves, cut them into 12-inch squares if necessary, discarding ribs, and steam for 20 minutes until soft and pliable. Toast chilies in a hot, dry skillet for 30–60 seconds, being careful not to burn them. Next, boil chilies in a minimum of water, covered, for 20 minutes. Remove stems. Remove seeds only if peppers are really hot. Puree chilies in a blender with onion, garlic, and tomatoes. Salt to taste. Combine sauce with raw pork and set aside.

Prepare corn mush by mixing all the ingredients in a large bowl, adding enough water to make a very soft dough, almost like thick batter. Assemble tamales: Open the banana leaf or cornhusk completely and spread corn mush into a rectangle in the center (about 4 inches by 3 inches and not more than ¼ inch thick). Add pork in sauce down the center. Fold corn mush over pork and fold the banana leaf or cornhusk tightly around it. You can tie string or a strip of leaf or husk around to hold it together. Stack tamales in a steamer and steam them for at least 1 hour, making sure there is always water on the bottom of your pot. Also, make sure tamales are not in direct contact with water. If you're using cornhusks, the easiest way to assemble the tamales is to lay the cornhusk smooth side up in front of you so it looks like the letter A. Then spread corn mush to about 1 inch from the left, right and lower edge. Stay at least 2 inches away from the top (narrow) edge. Fold tamale from right to left or from left to right. Last, fold the top of the A over the tamale as a flap. Stack tamales vertically with flap side down so fillings don't fall out. The easiest way to do this, if you have a steamer basket, is to place the basket on its side as you assemble and stack tamales. Some cornhusks are very small and difficult to use. You can glue two smaller husks together with a thin strip of corn mush.

Shrimp in Garlic Sauce

The vinegar in this recipe will relieve some of the heat from the peppers, which should be rather hot. The sauce will be fairly liquid, so the rice you serve this over will play the main role in the meal.

Serves 8

1 pound fresh hot peppers (such as jalapeños)
1 pound tomatoes
1 head garlic, peeled
¼ cup white distilled vinegar
2 pounds shrimp, peeled and deveined
¼ cup oil
Salt to taste

Remove stems and seeds from peppers and puree them with tomatoes, garlic, and vinegar in a blender as if you were making gazpacho. Fry shrimp separately in oil until done. Add pepper puree and salt and simmer for 5 minutes. Serve over rice.

Mexican Meringue Frosting

This is an easy frosting that seems magical because you don't have to mess with candy thermometers and complicated ingredients—just egg whites, sugar, and water! You can flavor the frosting by adding a couple of teaspoons of lemon juice or vanilla at the end, or up to a teaspoon of some kind of concentrated flavoring or extract. You can also color this frosting, which is pure white to begin with.

Frosts a large 12-inch by 18-inch cake

1½ cups sugar
½ cup water
6 egg whites

Add water to sugar in a heavy saucepan. Bring to a boil and simmer until syrup falls from a spoon in one continuous thread without dripping. It will basically be at soft-ball stage. When syrup gets close to done, beat egg whites until stiff. When syrup is ready, pour into egg whites in a thin, steady stream while continuing to whip egg whites. Continue to whip for several minutes until frosting cools. Use immediately.

A Fisherman's Wife

"Who knew that spinach did not grow in a can? I didn't. Really."

Jacquelyn Michelle Gibson-Clark

BORN
1976 in Pasadena, Texas

NEIGHBORHOOD
Central City

OCCUPATION
Marketing

HOLY TRINITY
Garlic, cayenne, olive oil

FISH?
For breakfast, lunch, and dinner!

JACQUI GIBSON-CLARK MARRIES UP IN THE FOOD CHAIN: "The way people talk about food here always leaves me with some sort of anticipation. In high school, people would be talking about a crawfish boil or what they were going to eat at Jazz Fest. We didn't talk about food in high school in Florida, because you just didn't talk about it. It was just food. But here it is something to look forward to, like, 'I can't wait for crawfish season.' What is springtime without a crawfish boil?

"I have lived here longer than my mom and the rest of my family because they left and went back to Florida. To me, Florida was never home. I lived there for fifteen years and it never felt like home. And I remember feeling that immediately here. I've just really sunk my teeth into this piece of the world.

"I always tried to make things at home. Quiche was the first researched dish I ever made. My mom thought it was creepy. Egg pie. I was maybe eleven or twelve, and nobody knew how to make a pie crust. My mom's mom, I called her. I was like, 'Grandmas know how to make pie crusts.' But she didn't, she was like, 'You go and you buy the mix.' So my mom went and got the ready-made that you roll out and you don't have to do anything to it, but I really wanted to, so I played with it for a long time, put flour on it and pinched it.

Jacqui and her husband, Sean, can eat fish and seafood three times a day. Hot crawfish for their wedding reception was a no-brainer. Sean goes fishing three or four times a week, or as often as Jacqui lets him.

"My dad's mom was this amazing Chinese food cook, for some reason. She would make her own dough for dumplings and make her own lo mein noodles and duck sauce. She was not playing around. She was really good at it. I shouldn't even say Chinese food; we called everything Asian Chinese. In the seventies it was sort of in vogue. That's kind of where my grandmother expressed herself a lot, was in food. And I can remember when she stopped cooking, or when it became a problem for her. She was just tired. And that is when she stopped really trying to express herself. She became very quiet, she watched a lot of TV, she stopped cooking.

"My father's brother's mother-in-law, her mother was a hundred years old and an amazing Louisiana cook. Momo was from Lake Arthur. When she was a little girl her father owned a grocery store and everybody had to work there, but he never let the girls have any money. And he was really abusive with them. So Momo used to pick cayenne peppers and dry them, and she had this cayenne pepper business that rescued her family, she and her mother, like liberated them.

"Before she died she had Mexican women cooking and she would sit there and be like, 'No! You're doing it wrong! That's not how you make a roux!' She would scream at them and she spoke real Cajuny, so they had no idea what she was saying. That part of my family, which isn't really my family, that's where people were interested in food. My family, like my mother's family, they don't get food. When my grandfather was in the hospital I went to the store and got fresh vegetables and pasta and started making this food, and my grandmother was like,

'Why would you waste your money on all this food?' And I was like, 'Well, you have to eat vegetables. You cannot eat pepperoni and cheese and smoke your Kools all day long.'

"Growing up with my mom, we ate raviolis. We ate canned food, frozen dinners, Weight Watchers, pizza, diet cola, Little Debbies. I definitely adopted a lot of my mom's weird food neurosis as a kid; it was really indulgent food and diet colas. Like, Alba shakes. You know about Alba shakes? It was like NutraSweet and cocoa that you mix with ice and water, and it was supposed to be some treat. My mom was always fretting about her weight and by extension mine. So we ate really unhealthy, and then we had to go on a diet and have Alba shakes and Weight Watchers.

"I hosted Thanksgiving one year, and I made corn bread stuffing with crawfish and andouille sausage and tasso, and it was really good and I was making the corn bread for the stuffing, and my mother was baffled. She was like, 'What are you doing? Can't you just get the mix or something?' They just think that food is work and you probably shouldn't eat it anyway.

"There's this idea in the world that women are good home cooks, but when a man goes out and cooks, then it's like an art. Like, 'You're a cook. I'm a chef!' I've worked with chefs who thought they were so fancy, and I don't think that's an appropriate way to relate to food. Food isn't about being fancy. That's the thing with New Orleans food. You don't have fancy people cooking fancy food here. They're poor people that are just working and cooking, and they're doing it well because food is important enough all by itself."

—As told by Jacqui Gibson-Clark

The Matrimony Meal

Jacqui and Sean had the following menu at their wedding reception:

Hot boiled crawfish with potatoes, corn, and whole heads of garlic

Crawfish phyllo pastries

Roasted duck on sweet potato biscuit with orange pepper sauce

Skordalia with spicy tomato relish on croustini

Salad of mixed greens with garnish of seasonal vegetables, spiced pecans, Pecorino Romano and Louisiana cane vinaigrette

Roasted root vegetable barley risotto with sherry and rosemary vinaigrette

Black-eyed peas with roasted garlic, wilted chard, kale and mustard greens, spicy carrot ribbon salad, and basmati rice

Cochon de lait

Cheese tray

Leidenheimer po-boy bread

Hazelnut carrot cake with Frangelico and white chocolate cream cheese icing

Bourbon chocolate cake

Crawfish Samosas

Perfect with leftovers from a crawfish boil! You'll need to peel about 3 pounds of hot, boiled crawfish to get 1 cup of tails. Jacqui serves her samosas with an eggplant dish that she makes with a dash of sherry and lots of olive oil. She also recommends serving them with sour cream mixed with fresh herbs. When she makes too much filling, she fries the rest with eggs for breakfast.

Makes 16

Dough:

2½ cups flour
½ teaspoon salt
1 cup buttermilk or yoghurt
4 tablespoons melted butter

Filling:

2 tablespoons butter
1 teaspoon spices, such as curry, cumin, and a dash of cayenne
½ cup chopped green onion
1 tablespoon minced garlic
1 cup (about ½ pound) crawfish tails, boiled and cleaned
4 small red potatoes, boiled and lightly crushed
1 tablespoon fresh herbs, such as oregano or thyme, chopped

For frying:

Peanut oil

Make the dough ahead of time so it can rest for a few hours. You can make a huge batch and freeze what you don't use. The dough is very resilient and comes in handy for both savory and sweet fried pastries. Simply combine all ingredients for dough. Knead with significant force until the dough reaches a stiff, rubbery consistency. Cover with plastic wrap and set aside. To make filling, heat butter in skillet. Add dry herbs, green onion, and garlic. Stir in crawfish and potato. Finish with fresh herbs and remove from heat. Assemble samosas by first rolling out and stretching dough until thin. Cut dough into large, even rounds using a yoghurt lid or something similar. Place a large spoonful of filling near the center of each circle. Carefully wet edges with water, using a pastry brush or your finger. Fold over and press edges together firmly. Let rest for about 30 minutes in the refrigerator. Heat oil in a pan suitable for deep-frying. Fry samosas until golden. Drain on newspaper topped with paper towels.

Fried Trout

Trout is a brittle fish, so it is important to have a sturdy batter to hold it all together. This is a 3-part dry-wet-dry batter that contains nutritional yeast: "I'm not sure it actually does anything, but I'm afraid to take it out." Jacqui usually serves her trout with a squeeze of fresh lemon and raw vegetables dressed in vinegar or citrus.

Serves 4

2 trout or 4 fillets
1 cup flour
½ teaspoon nutritional yeast
½ teaspoon + ½ teaspoon kosher salt

½ teaspoon + ½ teaspoon garlic salt

½ teaspoon + ½ teaspoon Tony Chachere's Creole Seasoning

½ teaspoon + ½ teaspoon cayenne pepper

2 eggs

1 sleeve saltine crackers, finely crushed

Cornmeal (about half the volume of crushed saltine crackers)

Peanut oil for frying

Fillet fish, if necessary. In one bowl, mix flour, nutritional yeast, and half a teaspoon each of kosher salt, garlic salt, Tony's, and cayenne. In another bowl, lightly beat eggs. In a third bowl, mix saltine cracker meal, cornmeal, and half a teaspoon each of kosher salt, garlic salt, Tony's, and cayenne. Heat oil in a pan suitable for deep-frying. Dunk each fillet into flour mixture, then eggs, then cracker mixture. Fry until golden. Drain on newspaper covered with paper towels.

Chocolate Cake

According to Jacqui, you can leave this cake on a rooftop for a week and it still will be moist and delicious. The batter is runny, so don't worry if you've made cakes before and this one seems different; you also put the sugar with the dry ingredients instead of mixing it with eggs or butter first. You will need at least 2 baking pans for this recipe, because it yields a lot and makes a high layer cake. Jacqui usually coats her cake with chocolate ganache and fills it with mousse, cream fillings, crushed chocolate espresso beans, or nothing at all. Raspberry jam is a good one too, but then you might want to add hot water instead of espresso to the cake mixture, or hot water mixed with brandy. The recipe is very versatile. You can use any hot liquid to enhance the flavor. And if you use affordable cocoa, this cake is cheap to make! (Author's note: Jacqui received this recipe from a friend and caterer who in turn received it from a chef. When I tried it and brought the cake to a birthday party, the hostess said that it reminded her of a recipe that she had gotten from the back of a cocoa box. Indeed, it's the same recipe, only doubled.)

4 eggs

2 cups milk

4 teaspoons vanilla extract

1 cup vegetable oil

4 cups sugar

1½ cups cocoa

3½ cups flour

1 tablespoon baking powder

1 tablespoon baking soda

2 teaspoons salt

2 cups hot liquid, such as espresso, coffee, or water

Beat eggs. Stir in milk, vanilla, and oil. In a separate bowl, whisk all dry ingredients together. Add wet to dry mixture. Stir in hot (!) liquid. Pour into 2 greased and floured baking pans and bake at 350 degrees for about 1 hour until a sharp, thin knife comes out clean when inserted into the center of each cake. Cool in pans for 10 minutes, and then turn cakes out onto a cooling rack.

Mama's Bad Boy

*"I haven't met anything
that I cannot eat yet."*

**WARREN BELL LEARNED FROM HIS MOTHER THAT FOOD IS WORTH ARGU-
ING OVER:** "My mother was such a dominant force that we didn't get to do much in the kitchen. I'm the oldest of seven, and my earliest memories of school was bragging to other kids about what I had for dinner, or how well we ate. We had a hot breakfast every morning before school; we were out the door with grits and eggs and whatever she decided we would have. She was amazing. Always a hot meal.

"My dad spent most of his career as a warehouseman for a supermarket chain. We always knew what the latest, newest foods were, and as soon as that paycheck would arrive he'd be at the grocery store spending most of it. Loading us up with things that most girls and boys in my class had never even heard of. I can remember saying, 'You mean, you never heard of a boneless rump roast?' My dad thought that food was very important.

"I probably don't cook as much as I should. I love to get the knives out. I love chopping seasoning and deciding whether I want to dice my bell pepper or have it in little strips. Do I want to sauté the onion or just put it in? In red beans, the rule is don't sauté the onions. In white beans, I sauté the onions. Why? Because that's how Mom said that I should do it.

Warren Anthony Bell, Jr.

BORN
1951 in New Orleans, Louisiana

NEIGHBORHOOD
Gentilly

OCCUPATION
Communications manager

HOLY TRINITY
Garlic, onion, bell pepper

ONLY IN NEW ORLEANS?
Liver, grits, and eggs

"I was sharing a story with one of the ladies at work this morning. My mom's the kind who will make something and when you say, 'Oh God, I love it,' your wife or one of the daughters-in-law will call and say, 'How did you make that?' And she'll tell them and then when they call back and say, 'I tried to make it but it didn't come out exactly . . . ,' she'll say, 'Oh, I don't do *that* anymore.' There's a little game she plays when she never truly tells you everything she puts into any recipe because she still has to be the dominant force, if you will.

Warren would cook beans every day if his wife, Rebecca, and their daughters would let him.

"Growing up, most of my exposure was to other relatives, and they all had the same ways of cooking as we did. When we left our house we went to other family members' houses, the typical New Orleans story. We rarely ventured out of our neighborhood. We stayed within the Treme area, or later on Gentilly.

"I think meals should be served at home. My wife said yesterday, 'A lot of people probably pick a place to eat out every day.' And I said, 'Yeah, but that's not us!' There is no way I would ever want that lifestyle. I have a friend in Baltimore that I visited recently. He got all excited and started grabbing the menus for all the take-out places so he could order a Philly cheese steak sandwich with me. It was a great meal, but I said, in New Orleans we would never dream of, 'Sit here while I order something for you to get delivered.' It would be, 'Hold on, let me see what I've got in the kitchen and let me fix something for you.' You have to be prepared to be hospitable even when company does not tell you it is coming.

"We are African Americans, but we are Afro-Creole here in New Orleans. My own family's background goes all over the globe and includes a very strong Sicilian presence. My grandmother's name was Colombo, and she didn't steal the name. She had blue eyes and long white hair until the day she died. So the Italian influence on what we do is very pronounced. We've always used tons of garlic in everything. My mother's meatballs are never just made of ground beef. It's ground beef with veal and a little bit of pork to give it that little bit of extra fatty content and flavor. Stuffed peppers have to be done differently from other folks. Yes, my Sicilian influence sings easily. You can put a cannoli in front of me and I'm a happy boy.

"My mom is very proud of herself as a cook. She always loved to watch cooking shows just to sort of say, 'Oh, I can do better than that!' It's not unlike what musicians do here with music. We call it jazz but I think the approach to cooking is very much an improvisational approach where we know what the classic dish is and it's not going to waiver too much, but on this day I might decide to add something just because making it different is the whole joy of fixing it. Again, being true to the melody, if you will. Giving each performance something a little different, depending on your mood and based on whatever fresh ingredients are available du jour. Jazz, cooking, it's all the same.

"With my mother, I've been in hot water more than once. There are a couple of things you never talk about. The bread pudding and the gumbo, you really shouldn't mess with her. There's been more than one Thanksgiving weekend when I was told, 'You know, your mom's mad at you for those comments you made in the kitchen.' 'But I said it was delicious!' 'Doesn't matter. You said *but*.' My sister tells me, 'Your problem is that you don't realize that you always have to say something, you can't just say it's good, you always have to add something and that's what she's mad at you for.' Guilty as charged. But I didn't steal it. I got it from her."

—*As told by Warren Bell*

Making Groceries at Schwegmann's

Two German brothers named Schwegmann opened a grocery store and bar at the corner of Piety and Burgundy streets in the Bywater neighborhood in 1869. It was the beginning of a supermarket empire. Schwegmann's was first to try self-service in New Orleans, offering a 10 percent discount to shoppers who helped themselves. The store on Old Gentilly Road was supposedly the biggest supermarket in the world at 155,000 square feet in the late 1950s. The chain was eventually sold in 1996.

Grilled Redfish

"It was my idea!" Warren grills his filleted redfish, when he can get one, skin side down with a Japanese-style marinade all around the fillets. The marinade is not an exact recipe. Warren often uses about ½ cup of teriyaki sauce, to which he adds garlic powder, Season-All, and soy sauce to taste. Depending on the sweetness of the teriyaki sauce, you might want to add 1 tablespoon of brown sugar. If it's very salty, skip the extra soy sauce and/or the Season-All. You can also add fresh, smashed and minced garlic and/or ginger to the marinade (3–4 cloves or a piece of ginger root the size of your thumb). Warren also suggests adding wine to the marinade and then reducing it in a saucepan on the stove to make it thicken up again. "Your favorite salad dressing would probably work fine too." So here is what you do: Gut the fish and remove the head and the tail. Split the fish in two, along the backbone, with a fillet knife. Remove backbone. You should now have two large fillets with skin and scales attached. Next, use your knife to separate the fillet from the skin from the tail toward the gills, leaving the gill end attached. Slather marinade between the skin and the fillet as well as on top of the fillet. When your charcoal grill is ready, place fish skin side down fairly close to the coals and cook until done, 10–15 minutes. It doesn't matter if you burn the skin, because you won't eat it anyhow.

White Beans

Warren uses baby limas, great northerns, or navy beans for this recipe. It doesn't matter. After simmering them with three kinds of pork for hours, they come out tasting about the same. He enjoys his beans on the brothy side and serves them over rice. "I don't chop my garlic, I smash my garlic, because somewhere along the way somebody said that's how you get the essence of the garlic to explode and disseminate more quickly."

Serves about 20

1 tablespoon olive oil
8 cloves garlic, smashed and coarsely chopped
4 onions, diced
1 red bell pepper, diced
2 pounds dried small white beans (soaked in water for 2 hours)
1 bunch green onions, chopped
1 gallon water (or slightly less)
1½ pounds pickled pork, cut into big logs
1 pound seasoning ham, cut into big chunks
1 pound fresh pig tails

Heat oil in a large pot. Sauté garlic and onion for a few minutes. Add bell pepper and sauté some more. Rinse white beans and add to pot. Add green onions and water. Bring beans to a boil. Add pickled pork and seasoning ham. Bring back to a boil and simmer, covered, for 1 hour. Add pig tails and cook until beans are soft and full of flavor, about another hour. If beans seem too brothy for your taste, leave the lid off. If pig tails start to fall apart, remove them and then put them back in the pot right before serving.

Mississippi River Masala

"I'm from the Mango Land."

KALPANA SAXENA FINDS A PLACE AT THE TABLE AMONG HER NEW ORLEANS BROTHERS AND SISTERS: "We were fascinated by food as little kids. I come from the city of Hyderabad, and everybody in India knows Hyderabad is like fabulous cooking, the most exotic. With my grandfather, every day you had a big breakfast, a big lunch, and a big dinner. And all this was very elaborate. Big menus and stuff. He would ask us what we wanted to eat, and the cooks would take the orders. My grandfather was in charge. He was a foodie. He was the biggest foodie of all time and a good cook himself.

"You started with breakfast, exotic at breakfast time. There was a dish called nehari, it's like a soup made out of lamb trotters and tongue. Trotters, you know, like the foot part of the lamb, they just removed some of the hooves and stuff. But oh man, was it a delicacy! This was a breakfast that we died for. See, you eat whatever you grow up with, like people eat pigs' feet over here. Nehari is cooked with cardamoms, vetivert, sandalwood, rose petals, and something called cassia. And, of course, you use coriander and cumin seed and all that stuff. It is cooked all night on a very slow fire, and the edges of the cover are sealed with dough so none of the steam escapes.

Kalpana Saxena

BORN
1957 in Hyderabad, India

NEIGHBORHOOD
Lower Garden District
(Lakefront pre-Katrina)

OCCUPATION
Lower school reading specialist

HOLY TRINITY
Onion, ginger, garlic

LOUISIANA BLUE CRABS?
With the green masala!

"Hyderabad did not belong to British India. The rulers of Hyderabad were descendents of the Moguls who were Muslim. So Hyderabad is a very interesting blend of Middle East and South Indian. Every sauce starts with frying the onions, ginger, garlic, and then you add these other spices into it, what I call masalas. The onions have to be very finely chopped because part of the Hyderabadi tradition is that you don't get these little pieces when you're chewing it. You're only supposed to chew the meat, not the masalas. You fry the onions until they are very golden, then you add the ginger and the garlic, and you keep frying it until you cannot smell that raw garlicky smell. Then you add your other masalas. You can't be in a hurry. You have to have time.

"We moved here in 1992. My husband got transferred. But we had been here earlier, so we were very excited to come here, because in all the places we went to in the U.S., this was the only place where we actually liked the food. We knew about red beans and rice, we knew about étouffée. It was very exciting.

"I first learned New Orleans cooking from cookbooks. Then once we started knowing people I started learning from them. This friend, a drummer, his mother taught me how to make shrimp stew. I learned to cook some things from her. I do the crawfish corn bread and greens New Orleans style, cooked with all those little bits of bacon and ham and whatever. Everything here is cooked with a lot of meat. That's another thing that is so common, I mean, in Hyderabad, there are just two or three vegetables that can be served as vegetables, the rest of the vegetables are combined with meat.

"My mother was here and she just fell for the food. She said, 'Oh, this is so good,' so now she cooks red beans and rice, but you don't get smoked sausage in India so she just uses whatever she gets, ham and salami. They also cook red beans the North Indian style with ginger, garlic, tomatoes, cumin powder, onions. She usually cooks it on a Monday after coming back from here. My dad's favorite dish in the whole world is fried fish, and the fish over here is the ultimate. He would get the best fried catfish in New Orleans East from a black guy on Chef Menteur. It was very fascinating, he served it on little toast, and my black friends explained to us that it's done that way because you don't want to see the grease. The toast soaks it up. They also liked the Vietnamese food here; they had never eaten Vietnamese before.

"Blacks call themselves brothers and sisters and we're already black and brown so we fit in anywhere. A friend tells me, you should go where the brothers go and I know exactly what they mean. Just how we like it. Turkey necks, I had never eaten a turkey neck in my life. The meat is very tender. And it's great fun picking it out. You can eat it like for half an hour, one neck! 'What are you doing?' 'I'm eating a turkey neck.' We started eating pig tails also. My black friends, when they make their red beans or white beans, they always make them with pig tails. It melts in the mouth. I think it's just fat. In Louisiana, they eat every part of a pig. The same thing in India. In Hyderabad, they eat every part of a goat. Even the tripe. We grew up eating liver and kidney and even brains with the green masala.

"I crave some of the dishes we ate as kids, exotic things that I don't know how to cook. There's a dish called muzbi and the people who cook it are Persian cooks, their ancestors came from Persia in the 1600s or something, so only they know how to cook this food and you have to hire their services. Muzbi is only found now in India. It's a whole lamb, they marinate the whole thing and then they stuff it. It's kind of like they make turkeys stuffed with ducks and chickens here, you know, that turducken? [Turducken, a deboned chicken stuffed in a deboned duck stuffed in a deboned turkey, is considered a Cajun specialty.] Muzbi is one of the most exotic and most

Kalpana celebrates Diwali, the Hindu festival of lights, preparing a huge feast for her New Orleans friends. Michael Kuhn and Maria Elliott want to know all about what they're eating.

exciting things I have ever had. So okay, the goat is stuffed with chickens. The chickens are stuffed with hard-boiled eggs. And then the masalas, it's unbelievable. They dig a hole in the ground and put burning coals around the dish, then they cover it with mud. When it comes out, all the meat is falling off the bones and the aroma hits you like a blast. You can just smell it and be happy.

"Everyone is a foodie over here. People are either dreaming of some food or some booze that they are going to have that evening. We're not embarrassed. People in New Orleans and people in Hyderabad are not embarrassed to admit that food is so important in their lives. My grandfather, you finished one meal, he would be arranging for what was going to be cooked for the next meal. Sometimes we were so full, we were like, 'Nana, please, we can't even tell you what we want to eat . . .' He was planning the next meal before the first one was over."

—*As told by Kalpana Saxena*

Crawfish Balls with Cilantro Chutney

This is Kalpana's favorite appetizer. You can substitute fresh mint leaves for cilantro, if you like.

1 onion, peeled and quartered

2 green bird's-eye chilies, stems and seeds removed

4 slices stale bread or up to ¼ cup breadcrumbs

1 teaspoon grated fresh ginger (or more to taste)

1 teaspoon finely minced garlic

2 pounds crawfish tails, peeled, with juice

1 egg, beaten

3 tablespoons tightly packed chopped cilantro

3 tablespoons chopped green onion

1 teaspoon hot red chili powder

Salt to taste (about 1 teaspoon)

Breadcrumbs for rolling

Chutney:

1 cup tightly packed chopped cilantro leaves

½ cup grated coconut

2 green bird's-eye chilies

6 cloves garlic

Juice of 1 or 2 limes

Sugar to taste

Salt to taste

Combine onion, chilies, bread (if used), ginger, and garlic in a food processor. Grind until smooth. Add crawfish tails and grind again. In a large mixing bowl, blend egg, cilantro, green onion, red chili powder, and salt. Add crawfish mixture and blend by hand. Add breadcrumbs (if used). Shape into balls the size of walnuts and roll in breadcrumbs. Bake for 20 minutes at 350 degrees. You can also flatten balls and fry them in butter in a pan until both sides are crisp and golden brown, or deep-fry them in oil. To make chutney: Grind together cilantro, coconut, chilies, and garlic to a paste in a food processor. Add lime juice, sugar, and salt. Serve, or bottle and refrigerate.

Diwali menu on her refrigerator, with magnets

Lima Beans with Shrimp

This recipe is easy to double or triple, if you're cooking for many. If you can't find hot red chili powder (sold in many Asian supermarkets), you can use cayenne. What is Kalpana's opinion about cayenne? "Lame!"

Serves 8

1 pound dried large lima beans
2 tablespoons vegetable oil
1 small tub of Creole mix seasonings (or about 2 cups finely diced onion, green onion, celery, green bell pepper, garlic, and parsley)
2 bay leaves
2 tablespoons pressed or mashed garlic
1 teaspoon hot red chili powder
2 teaspoons cumin powder
½ cup tomato paste
1½ pounds cleaned, deveined shrimp
Salt to taste
Fresh cilantro

Wash and soak beans overnight. Heat oil in a pan. Add Creole mix and bay leaves and sauté until slightly golden. Add garlic, chili, cumin, tomato paste, and ½ cup water. Stir until you see bubbles. Add beans and enough water to cover beans. Cover and cook on low heat for about 2 hours. When beans are soft, add shrimp. Cover and cook for 5 minutes. Add salt. Serve over rice and garnish with chopped cilantro.

Chicken Casserole

With bell pepper rings on top, this comes out looking a bit like that "exotic dish" your mother or grandmother made in the 1950s.

Serves 4

Olive oil
4 boneless skinless chicken thighs or breasts
1 cup sliced mushrooms
1 (11-ounce) can Green Giant white shoepeg corn
1 tablespoon sambar powder (Kalpana uses 2 tablespoons)
1 bell pepper cut into rings
1 can cream of mushroom soup
½ cup water
Fresh cilantro

Coat an iron skillet with olive oil. Brown the chicken 2 minutes on each side. Arrange in a baking dish. Put the mushrooms and corn over and around the chicken. Sprinkle sambar powder over everything. Arrange bell pepper rings on top. Thin cream of mushroom soup with water and spread evenly on top. Bake at 350 degrees for 30–40 minutes or until done. Garnish with chopped cilantro leaves.

Coffee and Oysters

"I'll eat anything that's fresh."

TOMMY WESTFELDT LIVES A HECTIC ROMANCE: "I tell you this. I wasn't allowed in the dining room until I was five years old. I always ended up eating in the kitchen along with the help. When I reached my fifth birthday I was allowed to have dinner in the dining room. I was so excited. It was like a graduation, you know, like a huge step for me.

"I remember my father and my mother always having coffee in the morning. I see them drinking coffee, so I wanted coffee. At first they never included me, allowed me to have it. But once I was very persistent and they gave me a little coffee with milk, and I thought that was great. Of course, a child looks at that as an adult adventure. And you sort of, as a child, you put yourself in that same class and it's an exciting moment. I was probably five or six. With milk.

"It's the same thing, as a child I would watch my mother and my grandmother eat oysters, raw oysters, and I kept saying that I wanted to try. 'No, no, you'll hate them.' I ate my first oyster and I loved it. Maybe I loved it because I was never allowed to eat it, but now I eat them all the time. I absolutely think they're great. I would go to the Pearl restaurant every time I visited with my father here at the coffee company. I would come down when I was either in high school or in college. Usually, I'd grab him—'Let's go have lunch and eat

Thomas Dugan Westfeldt II

BORN
1951 in New Orleans, Louisiana

NEIGHBORHOOD
Garden District

OCCUPATION
Green coffee importer,
Rex carnival organization official,
Honorary Consul of Sweden

HOLY TRINITY
Tabasco, butter, Worcestershire sauce

LIMIT?
Five cups!

oysters, raw oysters.' He loved them and I loved them. It was a time for us to bond together, I guess. It was a time for me to ask for whatever I needed, and it was also a relaxing time for both of us, so we could do that.

"When I was a child, the help did most of the cooking. My mother never really cooked, except for breakfast. She did a great breakfast. I mean; she would always fix us pancakes or waffles. Or we would have some extra quail or dove left over from dinner; she would have quail or dove on toast. Really nice

Albert Barrientos, Jr., has worked with four generations of Westfeldts: Tommy's grandfather, Tommy's father, Tommy, and Tommy's daughter. Every day, they "cup" (i.e., taste) at least nine types of coffee, deciding which beans to import. Albert's continued presence is important to Tommy, who sits on thirteen different boards of trade and civic organizations.

breakfasts. And dinners, she would normally have our help cook dinner. Some of the things I didn't particularly care for. Cow's tongue, I could have gone without. She liked that. Liver, she'd love liver. I wasn't too fond of that. But Mondays we'd normally have red beans and rice, that was a tradition, and now it's on the menus. As a child, I became very close to the help. Basically, they raised me.

"These days we cook, or my wife does. Sometimes our maid does, our Spanish maid does, depending on what we ask her to do. But mainly my wife and I do the cooking. Something I eat a lot is artichokes; I love artichokes. I'd eat them all the time if I could. Boiled, I boil artichokes and eat them with lemon and butter. I'll boil four or five of them and keep them in the refrigerator, eat them cold. In fact, I had one today for lunch.

"I kind of picked up cooking by myself. I love to cook. I don't have a lot of time to do it, cooking requires a lot of time, if you really want to cook well. I love to barbecue. I usually do that

on Sundays and have all the kids come home and have dinner. It's a good time for us to get together.

"The other thing I cook is duck. I love duck. I usually cook it in the oven, very slow, and I make sure that the duck is always moist. That's the key. You can do that by wrapping it in bacon or by continually basting it. Oranges is another great way to cook duck. It really comes out nice. The other way I cook duck is I barbecue it and smoke it for about three hours. You pick these things up. You go to somebody's house in New Orleans and you pick up that or you pick up this. I was doing it by trial and error, basically. I've gotten down to it pretty good.

"When you go into coffee, it's kind of a romance. We cup coffee every day, all different types of coffee. Once you cup a

To the Bitter End

Chicory coffee runs in high doses through the bloodstreams of south Louisiana, and has for generations. Chicory may be considered a roadside weed in most places, but in New Orleans it gives coffee that special taste that locals crave, smoky and slightly bitter. In the eighteenth century, Haiti (then a French colony called St. Domingue) produced half of the world's coffee. But after the 1791 revolution, Parisians and New Orleanians turned to chicory to stretch the divine drops. New Orleans's coffee culture was all the while much reinforced by the slave revolt, since the city soon hosted thousands of Haitian refugees. Rose Nicaud, a free woman of color, was reputedly the first person to serve demitasse to French Market shoppers and vendors. Gardner's city directory from 1859 lists about five hundred local coffeehouses. Some were combined with other businesses, such

as groceries (thirty-six) and boardinghouses (thirteen). There was even a "coffee house and wood yard" by the levee at Thalia and a "coffee house and wine store" at 34 Main (Dumaine) in the French Quarter, owned by an Italian. Today's clustering of coffee shops has nothing on New Orleans in the 1850s, where one could choose from five different coffeehouses just at the intersection of Magazine and St. Mary, twelve on St. Philip, and thirty-four along Tchoupitoulas. Café du Monde opened in the French Quarter in 1862, offering café au lait and beignets. It soon got competition from the Morning Call serving the same thing around the corner. Since the Morning Call relocated to Metairie in 1974, Café du Monde reigns supreme, adding a liberal sprinkle of powdered sugar on tourists ("Where is the menu?") and local regulars.

coffee, you get into all kinds of descriptions of coffee, like the coffee has a winey taste to it, which is good, or it's got a sweet taste to it, it's got body, meaning that it's thick, like a good cabernet, or it's thin or it has acidity. Those are all good characteristics. I think because of coffee, I've enjoyed, really enjoyed tasting different wines. I think my palate, thanks to coffee, is able to pick up the various different flavors. I love doing that.

"We sell chicory. It's very bitter but people love it. In the whole southern part of Louisiana, people, you ask them what they like to drink; they'll tell you coffee and chicory, dark roast with chicory. They grew up that way and it's just carried on. Here, a demitasse is basically strong chicory coffee. I remember my parents drank it every night before they went to bed. Strong, black coffee. They used to serve coffee and chicory in the office every day at two o'clock. A gentleman would come around and serve coffee on a silver tray with china cups. We don't do that anymore because we don't have enough help, and I would probably be the one serving the coffee."

—*As told by Tommy Westfeldt*

Ojen Cocktail

This is Tommy's pink party drink from Christmas to Mardi Gras. "It tastes like absinthe, and absinthe was a big deal here in New Orleans. My father used to drink Ojen all the time. It's a happy drink, puts you in a great mood. It's pink. I drink it all the time, every Mardi Gras and Christmas, the various different lunches."

Ice
2 ounces Ojen anise liqueur
4–6 dashes of Peychaud's Bitters
Club soda

Fill a short cocktail glass with ice. Pour Ojen over ice, adding bitters. Top off with club soda. Swizzle.

Mother-in-Law Meatballs

Tommy's mother-in-law, Shirley W. Hawthorne, got this recipe from a family in New Orleans in the 1950s and makes it every time her five children and in-laws come to visit. They are Tommy's favorite and bring to mind the New Orleans saying "So good I had to kiss my mother-in-law just to get the taste out of my mouth!"

2 slices French bread, 1 inch thick
Milk
1½ pounds ground beef
5 ounces grated Romano cheese
2 cloves garlic, finely chopped

¾ cup chopped yellow onion (about 1 onion)
¼ cup tomato ketchup
2 tablespoons flour
2 eggs
¼ cup finely chopped parsley
1 teaspoon salt
Flour for rolling

Preheat oven to 350 degrees and soak the bread in milk barely to cover. Combine and mix with a fork: ground beef, cheese, garlic, onion, ketchup, and flour. Beat eggs and add to meat. Press out excess milk from bread, and add bread to meat. Add parsley and salt. Shape the meat into 1½-inch balls. Roll each ball in flour. Place on cookie sheet. Bake uncovered about 30 minutes, or until browned. (Author's note: Shirley makes a fairly simple tomato gravy with equal parts canned tomato sauce and water, adding fresh parsley, salt, and all the drippings from the cookie sheet. She sinks the browned meatballs into the simmering gravy and serves them over boiled spaghetti.)

Café Brulot

Tommy makes this around Christmastime to warm himself before a duck hunt. "It's fun to light the bowl on fire and watch everybody squirm."

Serves 4

2 tablespoons chocolate syrup
2 cinnamon sticks
8 whole cloves
Large strip fresh orange peel
Large strip fresh lemon peel
4 ounces cognac, warmed
10 pieces lump sugar
2 cups hot, strong coffee

Place all ingredients except cognac and coffee in a large bowl that can withstand considerable heat. Add cognac, light the whole thing on fire, and stir ingredients slowly. After about 30 seconds, slowly pour in coffee. Stir. To serve, strain coffee into demitasse cups.

Singing Sunday Dinner

"Eat breakfast like a king, lunch like a prince, and supper like a beggar."

Marietta Esther Schleh Herr

BORN
1930 in New Orleans, Louisiana

NEIGHBORHOOD
Harahan

OCCUPATION
Homemaker

HOLY TRINITY
Onion, celery, garlic

COLLECTION?
48 beer steins

MARIETTA HERR COMPOSES HER MEALS IN THE GERMAN TRADITION: "There were no German groceries when I grew up, but we had Solari's. Solari's was an institution here. It was right off Canal Street in the French Quarter. My mother would go nearly every Saturday, and we were dragged along. They had herring in big barrels. They had all kinds of delicacies from all over the world. I remember that. They had the best food from Germany before World War II. And my mama had Langenstein's grocery, they still had barrels of salted herring, which my mother had to soak in order to get the salt out, several days in milk. And we had several bakers around that sold German bread, until recently. Mr. Kleindienst was the last one I knew. He was one of the few people who made rye bread without seeds, so people with diverticulitis would always go to get Mr. Kleindienst's bread.

"Schwegmann's carried a lot of German stuff. They even carried rabbits you could make hasenpfeffer out of. Hasenpfeffer, that's rabbit stew. They had one grocery, Kleinpeter's, that's a German name, and they carried rabbits. But when they closed, I didn't know where to buy them anymore. I miss them. Yes, I do. My brother-in-law would give us rabbits; he was a hunter up in north Louisiana. Since he died, I haven't had a rabbit.

German music was always part of the meal in Marietta's family. Her playing and singing were sweet desserts to be shared by all.

"The hamburgers, the breaded meat, the schnitzel, and the hot dogs, all are part of everyday cooking and not identified as German. That's become so Americanized, you don't consider that an ethnic food. Breaded meat here was a staple. I don't know if that came from Germany or not, but that's a schnitzel.

"The German culture was absorbed by the city. Especially after the two world wars. Our friend Charles Weber claimed during the war that he was English. He had two German parents; he was no more English than I was, but this is what happens when you want to get jobs. After Hitler, you know, German reputation really suffered.

"They had one German restaurant, Kolb's, and when they closed there were none. I didn't go there often. In fact, when my brother and sister-in-law were married, we had sauerbraten at Kolb's. And they put, instead of making it with cloves, they put cinnamon in there. I said, 'God, who did this?' You don't put cinnamon in sauerbraten, but that's what they had in it, and I said to Richard, my husband, 'I never want to go back there.' The spices are ginger, cloves, peppercorns, bay leaves—but no cinnamon. I thought to myself, 'Oh gee.' The red cabbage too had cinnamon! Somebody just didn't know.

"The German chefs, now, do not cook German food. They have this newfangled food that they're cooking. For instance, vegetables, they stir-fry something, or steam it. I mean, the old Creole food, like the old German food, red cabbage, you can't make that in a stir-fry, that takes a long time to get right. Sauerbraten takes a long time. All the foods that are now, you see them on television; you can do it in thirty minutes. *Pfuff*, that's it. Food like the old-fashioned is very difficult to find. Baked eggplant or baked mirliton, that's not that commonplace anymore. The new restaurants, they don't overcook their vegetables, they say. They're practically raw.

"We like Italian food, most Germans do. We like tomato gravies. And we ate plenty salads. Iceberg lettuce or endive salad. And we mixed the salad with potatoes and cucumbers; nearly all our salads were mixed with potatoes. And I still like to do that, especially cucumbers in potato salad, love that.

"I learned to cook from my mother and my mother-in-law. My mother-in-law was of German extraction and a wonderful Creole cook. She cooked gumbos, stuffed crabs, and crawfish bisque, which nobody makes anymore. It's too much trouble.

"My mother was big on modesty. She didn't like too much salt. Pepper or salt. But I like a lot of spices and salt. I got to like it. I put Tabasco on just about everything.

"My mother made spätzle with a bowl, by hand. She prided herself on how long they were. The bowl was in one hand and then she had to cut them with a knife in the other, and then she had to rotate the bowl at the same time, make each one indi-vidually. They're boiled. You drop them into the boiling water. It's like a noodle. Then you can fry them in egg, or just fry them in butter. Spätzle was her pride. They were her claim to fame. I say that jokingly, but it was. She really didn't try to teach me how to do that. And here is a strange thing. She liked to make them but she never ate them. She'd rather eat potatoes. Figures. She ate potatoes and bread. I think she liked the butter on them. We had a cow and she made her own butter. The fresh butter to put on the potatoes, that is good. She was big on butter. Ah.

"Butter is good for you. No matter what they say."

—As told by Marietta Herr

New Orleans Saved by Germans

Had it not been for Germans, New Orleans might have starved to death. After Bienville founded the Crescent City in 1718, the new French colony attracted more tradespeople, convicts, and soldiers than farmers. Hunger was a constant threat until John Law lured hundreds upon hundreds of German peasants to board ships to come here and settle what became known as *La Côte des Allemands*, the German Coast, referring to the Mississippi River bank upriver from New Orleans. By 1850, German-born outnumbered French-born in New Orleans. They remained the largest foreign-born, non-English-speaking group until large numbers of Sicilians arrived around 1900. Many of New Orleans's Germans were bakers, dairymen, and butchers. Anti-German sentiment after the two world wars led many to change their names and do away with cultural practices. German food is often mistakenly called Dutch, since *Deutsch* ("German" in German) and Dutch ("from the Netherlands") are easily confused. New Orleans's most famous German restaurant, Kolb's on St. Charles Avenue, invited guests to have Dutch apple pie in their Dutch Room before they eventually closed in 1994.

Sour Cream and Onion Pie (Zwiebelkuchen)

This is great party food, good both hot and at room temperature. "It's like a pizza."

Dough:
4 cups unbleached flour
1 teaspoon sugar
1 tablespoon active dry yeast
1 cup warm milk
1 teaspoon salt
2 eggs
1 stick butter, softened

Topping:
8 yellow onions, thinly sliced
½ stick butter
¼ pound ham, diced
2 cups sour cream
3 or 4 eggs
Salt to taste

Mix 1 cup of the flour with sugar and yeast. Add warm milk, mix well, and let rise for about 30 minutes. Lightly beat eggs and add to dough. Mix in salt, butter, and the rest of the flour. Beat dough in bowl for about 5 minutes by hand. Let dough rise, covered by a damp cloth, in a warm place until it has doubled in size. While dough is rising, sauté onions in butter. Lightly beat eggs and add to sour cream. Mix all ingredients for the topping except for the ham. Roll out dough like a pizza and place on a large, oiled cookie sheet. Cover with topping, sprinkle with ham. Bake at 400 degrees for about 40 minutes.

Marinated Pot Roast (Sauerbraten)

Start almost a week in advance! Serve with potato dumplings, spätzle, other noodles, or mashed potatoes.

Serves 8–10

4 pounds chuck roast

For marinade:
1 cup water
2 cups red wine vinegar
3 cups cider vinegar
1 large onion, minced
1–2 cloves garlic, mashed
6 black peppercorns
8 whole cloves
8 whole allspice
2 bay leaves
2 carrots, peeled and sliced
Small piece fresh ginger, peeled and bruised
A few mustard seeds
A few sprigs fresh parsley, broken up
2–3 ribs celery, in pieces
1 lemon, quartered
1 tablespoon Worcestershire sauce

For roasting:
4 tablespoons bacon fat
2 onions, sliced
4 whole cloves
1 bay leaf

For gravy:

3 tablespoons butter

3 tablespoons flour

1 tablespoon brown sugar

3 tablespoons sour cream

Salt and pepper

Mix together all the ingredients for the marinade in a pot, pressing the juice out of the lemon. Bring to a boil. Simmer for a few minutes. Cool and pour over meat, covering it in marinade. Marinate for 5 days in the refrigerator, turning meat once or twice a day with hands. Remove meat from marinade and brown in bacon fat with onion slices in a Dutch oven. Strain marinade (discarding all solids) and add enough to meat to immerse half. Add cloves and bay leaf. Simmer on low for about 4 hours, turning meat periodically. Transfer roast to serving platter. Strain gravy and discard onions, etc. Melt butter in a pan, adding flour and sugar to make a roux. Add gravy to flour mixture very slowly and stir until smooth. Add sour cream, salt, and pepper to taste. Serve gravy in a gravy boat.

Beer stein

Red Cabbage (Rotkohl or Blaukraut)

It is not unusual to find brown sugar in recipes for red cabbage, but Marietta cannot stand the taste. "The onion and apple is sweet enough!" Red cabbage is usually served with sauerbraten.

Serves 8–10

1 small red cabbage

¼ cup canola oil

1 small yellow onion, thinly sliced

1 small yellow apple, peeled and grated

1 cup red wine, or wine and water mixed

¼ teaspoon ground cloves

Juice of 1 small lemon

Salt

Remove outer leaves and cut cabbage into quarter sections. Remove core, then shred cabbage. Sauté onion in oil until transparent. Add apple and cabbage. Stir in about half the red wine. Add cloves. Cover pot and braise slowly for 10–15 minutes, then add the rest of the wine. Cook, covered, until cabbage is soft, about 45 minutes. Check often and add water if cabbage seems dry and sticks to the bottom of the pot. Sprinkle with salt to taste and add lemon juice to bring out the red color just before serving.

Joy Wok Club

"Trial and error, that's how we found out how to do things."

YO CHIN COOKS CATFISH, JAMBALAYA, AND PRETTY MUCH EVERYTHING IN A WOK: "I'm a connoisseur of hot dogs. I've eaten every one. Everywhere we go I look for hot dogs. I've always liked them. It's easy to eat, quick, simple. That's it. I'd rather eat something plain every day.

"We have several hot dog cookers. We have the kind that electrocutes them. You stick the hot dog in and you plug it in and electricity runs through it and literally electrocutes the hot dog. We have one of those. Then we have the hot dog machine with the rollers. What else? We steam it, or over open gas fire, cook it like that.

"I grew up behind St. Joseph Church, on Gravier and South Roman. My dad had a laundry there. The original Chinatown was a little further down, Gravier and Loyola, maybe four blocks away, in that area. I came over when I was four years old.

"My grandpa was here first. He came over, I believe, in 1909. He was in the dried shrimp business. The company was actually one of the first shrimp companies in the United States that he got involved with. We had dried shrimp platforms down on Grand Isle, right off of Grand Isle, and then they had some

Yeu Jwo "Yo" Chin

BORN
1948 in Kwangtung, China

LIVES IN
Metairie

OCCUPATION
Cook
(makes soups at local coffee shop)

HOLY TRINITY
Onion, garlic, ginger

EATING RECORD?
216 dumplings!

Yo Chin brings out eight giant woks when it's time for the Men's Club to fry catfish and French fries at St. Angela Merici three times a year.

older ones, I don't know exactly where. My dad, he ran one of the platforms, and then my brother wound up going there.

"I was in Manila village, Barataria Bay, when they had the platforms and all that. I was a little kid then. That's where I ate my first raw oyster. We got it right out the bayou. My dad and my grandpa danced the shrimp. The shrimp would be dried, they boiled the shrimp in salt water and then they'd put it out in the sun to dry. After a day, this is before they had the machines to tumble shrimp to get the shells and the heads off, so they had to go out there and walk and dance on the shrimp. Then you take the shrimp and you use these big baskets and toss it in the air like they do with rice, let the wind blow the shells away and you're left with shrimp. They'd bring it to town and ship it to China back in the old days.

"The only American dish my dad ever made was turkey, which, he always believed in high temperature. With Chinese cooking, you use a lot of heat. We roast duck at four hundred and fifty or five hundred degrees. But then, after a while, he forgot it, read the newspaper and all that, so we never really ate turkey. That's when I decided to take over cooking the Thanksgiving bird and all that. I was fifteen years old. But he cooked steaks, marinated with soy sauce, or my mother would always cook chicken. We had soup and rice every night, basically the same thing, it didn't bother me. Mother made oyster stuffing for the turkey. My dad told her and she just put it together. For years, that's all we ate because Dad always burned the turkey.

"In China there's no refrigeration. My mother used to leave food out on the table all the time. It was hard for her to accept using the refrigerator. But she basically ate pretty well here. My dad would bring shrimp. I mean; I learned to eat oatmeal with dried shrimp. And that's the only way I eat it. I won't eat it sweet. I eat it with dried shrimp.

"When my kids used to say they're hungry, I'd tell them, 'Go talk to your grandma and she'll tell you what hunger is really like.' She went through the war, and she always had a hatred for the Japanese because when they came through they took everything. My mother said, 'Can you imagine trying to survive with a bowl of rice for five people for a week?' Basically, that's what they had, and they stole the equipment. How do you cook without pots? Utensils? So she could tell you what plants are edible, what aren't. She even ate roaches and mice and all that. I told the kids, 'Talk to your grandma. She'll tell you what it's like to be really hungry.'

"I've adapted Chinese cooking with American cooking. Instead of making a roux, I use dark soy sauce and cornstarch. I don't have to waste my time with the roux. If I have to make a roux, I use my wok and high heat, throw the flour in and it's done. Those are little tricks, and a lot of people can't tell the difference.

"I like my red beans and rice with pig tails. I cook the pig tails separate and then I mix with my red beans and rice. We make gumbo. Sometimes we make seafood gumbo with crabs, shrimp, oysters. Then we make a chicken and sausage gumbo, that's about it. I cook jambalaya sometimes, for the Men's Club here. In a wok. I can get the high heat real quick and then turn it down, let the rice cook slowly. Camping, I've taught my second son, I learned it from my mother, instead of waiting for the fire to die down, you use the embers. He can sauté whatever he wants to sauté. He's cooked shrimp étouffée on a campout. We've fried chicken on a campout. It saves a lot of wood. And with a wok you can cook for a lot more people than with regular pots."

—*As told by Yo Chin*

"Ho See for Ho-Hum"

Yo's grandfather was featured in *Newsweek* in 1942, as a pioneer of the sun-dried oyster business in America, at Grand Isle, after the Japanese stopped dried oyster (ho see) exports from China. The media attention was difficult. Yo remembers, "My grandfather was always afraid of being deported because he came over in a box. He and one of my great-uncles hid themselves in a box. They didn't have enough food to last the whole trip, so they wound up eating this Chinese medicine. Chinese medicine used to be encased in wax, like a golf ball, and the medicine is inside. They ate the medicine. And then they ate the wax."

Sweet and Sour Shrimp

Fried shrimp that stay crunchy even when smothered in sauce! If you like soft-shell crabs, you can fry some of those up too.

Serves 8

1½ pounds large peeled and deveined shrimp
Salt and pepper
Vegetable or peanut oil for deep-frying

Sauce:

1¼ cups sugar
1 teaspoon ginger powder or fresh, grated ginger to taste
2 carrots, peeled and grated
1 green bell pepper in thin slivers
1 (8-ounce) can crushed pineapple
¾ cup cider vinegar
1½ cups water
2 tablespoons cornstarch

Batter:

1 cup flour
½ cup cornstarch
2 teaspoons baking powder
1½ cups water (start with less, add more if needed)

Prepare sauce: Mix cornstarch with a couple of tablespoons of the water and set aside. Combine all other ingredients in a large pot and bring to a boil over medium heat. Add cornstarch and simmer for a few minutes. Set aside. Prepare batter: Mix the dry ingredients first. Add water slowly, stirring batter with a fork until smooth and resembling pancake batter or yoghurt. Heat oil to 325 degrees in a wide pan deep enough for deep-frying. Season shrimp with salt and pepper. Drop them into batter until well coated and then drop about 6 shrimp at a time into hot oil. Fry until batter hardens and turns golden, 1–3 minutes. Place fried shrimp on a platter and pour warm sauce over them. Serve with white rice.

Ho See for Ho-Hum

Ho see, or dried oysters, is the Chinese sulphur and molasses. Cooked up in a soup with soybean paste or Chinese pumpkin, *ho see* is a springtime tonic guaranteed to relieve that feeling of ho-hum.

Chinese-Americans once imported the tonic from Southern China—an area now also looks to the sou[t] its first shipment t[o] Zone. But if the Lo[u] pand much further, problem: American tery than the Orien[t] less *ho see* on dryi[ng] Quong Sun may ado[pt] partially drying the them in oil.

Oysters shrink like this when they're dried fo[r]

Newsweek

Pigs in a Cloud/Steamed Pork Buns (Bao)

Yo's wife, Dixie, usually makes these.

Makes 16 large or 24 medium buns

Filling:

1½ pounds roast pork (shredded or diced)

1 bunch green onions, chopped

⅔ cup oyster sauce

4 tablespoons sugar

Dough:

2 pounds flour

1 cup sugar

¼ cup vegetable shortening

1 cup water

1 cup milk

1 envelope yeast

Mix all ingredients for the filling, cover, and set aside. Prepare the dough: Mix flour and sugar in a large bowl. Add shortening, using hands to make it disappear into the flour mixture. Warm the water and milk (about the temperature of a nice bath) to dissolve and activate the yeast. Add yeast liquid to flour mixture. Knead dough until blended and soft. Shape dough into a round ball, cover with a damp cloth, and put in a warm place to rise for 1 hour. Punch down dough, knead again, cover with cloth, and let rise again, about 30 minutes. Knead dough and divide into 16 or 24 balls. Flatten balls into circles with a rolling pin. Put a spoonful of the filling in the center of each circle. Bring dough around filling, enclosing it com-pletely, pinching to close buns. Place buns, seam side down, on small pieces of wax paper. Let rise, covered, about 30 minutes. Cook buns in a steamer for about 15 minutes. Serve hot or at room temperature.

Oyster Sauce Marinated Steaks

This is an easy recipe to bring to a potluck barbecue, or if you go camping.

Steaks

Black pepper

Garlic powder

Premium Brand oyster sauce

Vegetable oil spray

Choose your cut of steaks (ribeye, t-bone, porterhouse) and place in a shallow pan. Season each side with black pepper, garlic powder, and 1 tablespoon oyster sauce, rubbing this into the meat. Set aside and marinate for 1 hour. Preheat grill (medium to high heat). Spray nonstick oil on grill. Cook steaks to your desired doneness.

A Chicken in Every Freezer

"'It takes a real coonass to figure out how much gravy it would take to cover a field of rice.' That's something Dad used to say."

THANIA MAE ELLIOTT'S HUSBAND SAYS SHE COOKS TOO MUCH: "I like to have people around. I do red beans and rice a lot because it's just so easy. The first Friday of Jazz Fest I've always had a red beans and rice night. Let's wind down from Jazz Fest and let's do that.

"Holidays, we divide them up. New Year's Eve has been my holiday, that's one of my favorite times. Hundred people would come. You'd have parents and children, dates and young people; my nephews would bring their friends. It was just a way for us all to be together and enjoy each other's company. People will say, 'It's like a wedding reception, I've never seen so much food.'

"To start, we always have a soup of some kind, chicken and sausage or shrimp gumbo. Roast. My husband always makes one or two hundred little finger sandwiches. You sort of always knew when you walked in what you were going to have. We always had the same routine. One punch bowl we'd have pineapple daiquiris, and on this side we'd have piña coladas, and in the middle it'd be champagne punch. Three big punch bowls; they knew that.

Thania Mae Elliott

BORN
1941 in Cameron, Louisiana

NEIGHBORHOOD
Lakeview

OCCUPATION
Nurse

HOLY TRINITY
Onion, celery, garlic

MOTTO?
Make more!

After putting out snacks and plates and paper towels, making macaroni and cheese, and bringing in the picnic table from the yard for the grandchildren, Thania sits down last to enjoy some spicy boiled shrimp, corn, potatoes, onions, and garlic with her family.

And I had a big dining room table, which we'd fill mostly with appetizers or sweets, and then the table in the breakfast room would have all the hot stuff. Sometimes it was too crowded, and we had to put the gumbo pot on the stove. You sort of had the limit based upon how much space we had on the surfaces. Lots and lots of food, solid food that you would eat. I can't imagine having a party and keeping people there without food.

"I'm the oldest of the three sisters here in New Orleans. I do have an older sister, she stayed in Cameron. She's still in Cameron, in fact. We went through Hurricane Audrey, a hurricane that destroyed Cameron Parish in 1957, and we lost three children. The whole town was wiped out almost. Our house went over. I floated away. I was in the water fourteen hours. That's why Katrina didn't bother us as much, because it was just property. All of us are coming back to Lakeview. Six blood relatives. Six houses.

"Family is the most important thing in the world. All my degrees, I have three different degrees, I've been to all these different colleges, my job's fairly nice, but that means nothing compared to family. I'd never put food up as high, but I can't think about family without having food as part of it. But as far as food as interest, no. Food is not my interest. Do I like to cook? Not necessarily. Do I like to eat? Not necessarily.

"I think everything we ever did was food centered. And I think that came from Mom. It wasn't like Mom had parties, but she always cooked lots and lots of food. It wouldn't be just a meat and two vegetables and a salad. It might be two meats, five vegetables, and a salad. Every day. 'Oh, we're like that because we're southern' or 'We're like that because we're Catholic' or 'We're like that because we're Cajun.' How do you know?

"I don't know what we did with leftovers, because Daddy didn't eat leftovers. We ate leftovers. The children did. Today, we all do. I use the freezer, I freeze things and then I pull them out later. I had a refrigerator in the kitchen, a large side-by-side. I had a refrigerator outside, large side-by-side with a freezer. We had a covered patio, that was your beer refrigerator. In New Orleans you have to have a beer refrigerator. Then I had a refrigerator in my utility room, and then I had two freezers. And everything was filled to the top. You could barely find space in there. Just my husband and I, we still had that many refrigerators and freezers. And see, when Mom and Dad died, I think she had three chest-type freezers, the big old long things like this. Two refrigerators and three gigantic deep freezers. And they filled them. In Cameron you butchered your own cows, so it'd be all in your freezer. They would buy shrimp, fifty or a hundred pounds at a time.

"What am I thinking about when I'm cooking? Probably that I'm going to have enough. Always my fear is that I'm not going to have enough. I'm always going to make just a little bit more, and my husband complains about that. He says I cook too much, but I don't want anybody to say they came to my house and didn't have enough food. That's where we have the conflicts. He's from Arkansas. See, my daddy would never have told my mama, 'You cook too much.' He'd always say, 'Cook more! Cook more!' But Bill is from Arkansas, and his concern is always that I cook too much. It's always the quantities. He says I'm going overboard. It could be maybe that's southern. Arkansas, I know it's in the South, but it's still not really Louisiana."

—*As told by Thania Mae Elliott*

Potato Salad in Gumbo

The tradition of eating potato salad with gumbo is sometimes called Cajun, sometimes German. Thania tells this story: "Mom and Daddy had potato salad in gumbo. When you served your bowl, you'd have rice, your gumbo, and then you'd take a thing of potato salad and put it on the edge of the bowl. That's a Cajun thing. Way back when, they used to put eggs in the gumbo. They would drop a raw egg into the gumbo and let it cook in there. Something about gumbo and eggs was the thing, I think. We always had potato salad."

Aunt Mae's Famous Chex Mix

There are, of course, hundreds of versions of this homemade snack. This one is sometimes called Texas Trash. People have been known to attend Thania's parties just to eat her Chex mix.

Makes 14 cups

3 cups Chex Wheat Cereal
3 cups Chex Corn Cereal
3 cups Chex Rice Cereal
3 cups mixed nuts (mainly pecans, peanuts)
2 cups pretzels, broken into pieces
1 stick unsalted butter
½ cup bacon fat
1 tablespoon Tony Chachere's Creole Seasoning
1 tablespoon garlic powder
1 teaspoon cayenne
2 tablespoons Worcestershire sauce

Put cereal, nuts, and pretzels in a large roasting pan. Melt butter and bacon fat in a saucepan. Add seasonings to fat. Pour seasoned fat over cereal mixture, stirring and coating well. Bake in the oven at 225–250 degrees for 1 hour or more, stirring every 15 minutes. Cool completely and store in air-tight containers.

Crawfish Étouffée

This recipe originally came from Thania's sister Gloria's late husband, Floyd Kelley, in Cameron. Now, all the sisters make it. "Make sure it's spicy," Thania says. "Crawfish étouffée has got to be spicy."

Serves 6–8

1 stick butter
2 large onions, diced
2 ribs celery, diced
2 cloves garlic, minced
1 green bell pepper, diced
1 bunch green onions, chopped
1 bunch parsley, chopped
2 tablespoons tomato paste
1–2 pounds crawfish tails
4 tablespoons flour
2 large or 4 small chicken bouillon cubes
2 cups hot water
Salt, pepper, and cayenne to taste

Melt butter in a large pot. Add chopped vegetables (yes, parsley is considered a *vegetable* here) and cook over low to medium heat for 30 minutes. Add tomato paste and mix well. Add crawfish tails and sauté for 5 minutes. Stir in flour. Dissolve bouillon cubes in water and add to pot. Simmer for 15 minutes and season to taste with salt, pepper, and cayenne. Serve over white rice.

Something for Everyone

"Sit straight. Use your napkin.
Blessings first."

AIDA GRAY KEEPS FAMILY AND NEIGHBORS COMING BACK FOR MORE:
"I learned to cook from my mother. It was not like her really teaching me, I always watched. I was always in the kitchen with her. We have a big family, so she would always cook for everyone. We'd have hampers of beans and lima beans, okra and stuff like that. Sacks of crawfish to make crawfish bisque. A whole table of mustard greens. Crates of pears. She would cook all of this for everybody and I'd be in there helping her, peel things and clean. So I just picked up all of her techniques, but I've learned shortcuts in my time.

"Once I cooked for five or six hundred people, a wedding, we have a big family. And my ex–mother-in-law, they have a big family so when you bring the two families together, you have some people. And then you have all this extended family, cousins that you've never met. Family and close friends, so you just get together and do it. Every holiday, they're here. Mother's Day is the only one I may go out.

"I always cook a lot and I put containers for everybody so they can pick their food up. I make something that everybody likes, so they enjoy their meal. I know what they want. I have a neighbor across the street who does not cook, so I cook enough so she has food for a couple of days. Saturday, I

Aida Margarete Gray

BORN
1948 in New Orleans, Louisiana

NEIGHBORHOOD
Broadmoor

OCCUPATION
Childcare provider

HOLY TRINITY
Celery, bell pepper, garlic

COOKING TIP?
Prepare!

may cook beans, do a meat loaf, meat sauce, I'll put pork chops in the oven, roast chicken, fix greens. I fix a whole lot of stuff on the weekends and put in containers, and that pretty much takes me through the week.

"I do not use salt. You have enough spices, enough seasoning. I mean, who needs another grain of salt? I stopped adding salt to my food thirty-four years ago.

"Rarely I write down a recipe. I have learned to cook how they cooked in my grandmother's era and her mother's. You use what you have and you don't waste anything. I like to experi-

Aida runs a day care out of her home, which has two kitchens. The kids eat everything she eats. Green beans, asparagus, okra. "Fussing is for home, controlling your parents. I'm in control here. They just eat, and ask for some more." Today, Abby and James Lawrence and Dequan Dwyer enjoy a large plate of cupcakes.

ment. I cook, but other people try it for me, they tell me how it is. When they come here, 'Hey, try this.' And they'll sit and eat it. 'What is it?' 'You don't want to know, just eat it.' 'That's good, what is it?' Then I'll tell 'em what's in it and it doesn't matter. Last month we had deer meat and I had the whole hindquarter, which I had never cooked before, so I just used a little imagination. I cleaned it and soaked it in the vinegar water and put it in the cooker. They ate it all.

"I plan my meals; make sure I have all my ingredients. I prep; have everything cut up and in containers. And I just have to pick up, pour in, and do what I have to do. That prevents you from making mistakes. Especially when you spend a lot of money on things that you're fixing. You cannot afford to make a mistake.

"I'm a firm believer in cleaning as you cook. Oh, I can't stand finishing cooking and have chaos. I'm washing and cleaning dishes as I'm going along. So when you finish you can sit down with everybody. Usually, for holidays, I start a week ahead of time, with the mirlitons, stuffing that and stuffing peppers. Doing all that a week ahead of time.

"When we get together we talk about everything. What has happened, the future and the past. We always talk about how my mama used to cook. Why don't I make teacakes or do like she does? It is loving times. In my life, it's always food bringing me with family. Friends and family, we always connect back together over food.

"I have an extended cousin who works for the IRS, who does my taxes. And she said, how much do I owe you, 'Cook me something.' Last year, her mom was dying and she was home and I sent crawfish bisque, and that was the last thing I can remember her eating, her mother, and how she enjoyed it. And my friend in Chicago, he's very sick, and his fondest memory when he comes here is when I bake chicken. So three weeks ago, I sent a chicken to Chicago and it was like I sent him a pot of gold. I've gotten thank-you notes and phone calls, and that's memory. You know, people nice to you and you being nice to them. I'm going to do some crawfish bisque for my tax person because I know she'll like that. And if I do a twice-baked potato and a steak and call her over for dinner, she's in hog's heaven.

"I'm just a cook. I mean; I love to cook."

—*As told by Aida Gray*

"Recipes for Today's Foods"

One of the most interesting recipe collections from New Orleans is *From Woodstoves to Microwaves: Cooking with Entergy*, sold through United Way. This book shows you how locals actually cooked, and still cook, at home. The recipes originally came with electric bills from NOPSI, New Orleans Public Service Inc., the predecessor to Entergy, starting in the late 1940s. Recipes were found on streetcars as well, as NOPSI also ran the transit system. Most recipes were organized under a theme, such as "Salads Supreme," "Plentiful Pecans," "Luncheon Ideas," "Recipes for Today's Foods," and "Lagniappe." The recipes call to mind at once standard 1950s American fare and very old New Orleans dishes. "Parade Foods" includes daube glacé and beignets, while "Foods with a Foreign Flavor" offers nine Italian (!) recipes, such as stuffed artichokes and braciuolini, and two French, veal cordon bleu and coq au vin. Of course, New Orleans cooking was nothing if not French and Italian. The NOPSI recipes also show that locals found use for American products such as cream of mushroom soup in recipes like flounder with crab sauce, crawfish pie, and mirliton casserole.

Seafood Meatballs

Aida usually serves her meatballs with a light gravy, which she makes with roux mix, water, crawfish juice, a shrimp bouillon cube, and pepper to taste. You can also deep-fry the meatballs, or form patties to fry in butter in a skillet.

Serves 8

1 pound shrimp, coarsely chopped
1 pound crabmeat, coarsely chopped
1 (1-pound) package crawfish tails, coarsely chopped (saving the juice for gravy)
1 small bell pepper, any color, finely chopped
1 yellow onion, finely chopped
1 rib celery, finely chopped
2 cloves garlic, finely chopped
1–2 tablespoons Paul Prudhomme's Seafood Magic
1 egg, beaten
½ cup breadcrumbs
Flour
Vegetable oil spray

Mix all ingredients except flour. Add enough breadcrumbs for the mixture to hold together. Let rest 30 minutes while breadcrumbs absorb moisture. Roll into balls with wet hands. Lightly flour meatballs. Spray a cookie sheet with oil and brown meatballs in oven at 400 degrees for about 30 minutes until golden. Serve with pasta, rice, or whatever you like.

German Potato Salad

This might be the best potato salad you've ever tasted. Feeds a crowd!

10 pounds red potatoes
2 pounds bacon
¼ cup flour
½ cup sugar
1 tablespoon salt
2 teaspoons celery seed
1 cup water
1⅓ cups balsamic vinegar
4 cups chopped celery
2 cups chopped red onion
1 pint Hellmann's mayonnaise

Peel potatoes and cut into small cubes, boil until tender but firm, drain, and set aside. Cook bacon, drain on paper towels, chop, and set aside. With bacon grease still in pan, add flour, sugar, salt, and celery seed to make a roux over medium heat for 2–3 minutes. Add water to roux, then vinegar. Turn off heat and cool. Mix everything. Serve warm or cold.

Drawing made by one of Aida's charges, Willa Richards.

Strutting with Some Barbecue

"I'm on the bottom of the totem pole as far as the level of cooking in my family."

RONALD LEWIS BUILDS HIS NICHE AROUND THE GRILL: "It's just everyday life, but people fall in love with the way I barbecue. I've got my way of putting my sauce together, my way of grilling my meat. That's just what I do. New Orleans is a place where everybody has found a niche with certain things that they cook. And with me, barbecuing is my niche. You know, in most African American homes, when you're growing up your parents are going to bring a certain level of survival cooking to you. Like my mama used to say, 'As long as you know how to cook rice and grits you will never be hungry.' So that's the first thing she taught us. My mother was from the country, she was from north Thibodaux, and they taught you how to fix food that will keep you going.

"I love barbecuing chicken wings and the Double D smoked sausage. I can do them two all day. Meat cooking in their natural juices, that's one flavor. With the sauce, which I do two sauces along with my own things to turn it up a notch. I use natural honey; I use Tabasco sauce, a little cayenne pepper, lemon. When you bite into that meat you have a lot of flavor. That's what I truly enjoy. It's like, 'No complaints.' After you do something so long it becomes like second nature along with how you prepare your sauce, how you

Ronald William Lewis

BORN
1951 in New Orleans, Louisiana

NEIGHBORHOOD
Lower Ninth Ward

OCCUPATION
Retired streetcar track repairman

HOLY TRINITY
Tabasco, barbecue sauce, honey

WHAT'S NEXT?
Lobster boil!

Ronald tells his sister-in-law, Chonia H. Taylor, and his brother-in-law, Leroy Gardner, how he once tried to grill a goat and didn't know to parboil it first. "That was one goat that was eaten alive!"

prepare your meats. Be consistent! If you try too hard to alter your sauces then you're looking for disaster, so you sort of try and stay consistent with the ingredients and flavors and stuff. You be around so many people who cook and everybody got their own way. You can watch what that person is doing to add into what you're already doing. It is certain tastes that I look for. You think that you know it all, but then somebody else knows a little bit more than you.

"My mother was one of those true country cooks. She made the biscuits from scratch, the tea cookies and the fried bread. None out the box. Here in the Lower Ninth Ward we used to have a garden in the yard. She grew her own bell peppers. She grew white and yellow corn, tomatoes and parsley and the hot peppers, the little shorty ones. She used a lot of stuff that she grew in her cooking. A lot of the people in the Lower Ninth Ward came out of either the Mississippi Delta or out of the sugar cane belt. So they brought their ways to this part of the city. It wasn't unusual to see gardens in people's backyards.

"My uncle who lived on a plantation all his life would kill a hog every fall. We would go out there early in the morning. They would gut him and clean him and disperse the meat. My mother would come back and make hog cracklings. She cooked wild game. Rabbits, raccoons, you name it, squirrels. Most people in this area cooked country in some way or another. Like the lady next door to us, Ms. Skipper, she used to make these crawfish bisques. We couldn't wait until Ms. Skipper made her crawfish bisque. She specialized in that. They had a lady a couple of houses down, Ms. Smith. Her baking, she made these cakes like second to none. Everybody knew her cakes. These are the things I hold the fondest memories about.

"We had cherry trees in the next block from us, and my mom would make cherry wine. Sometimes, we'd be sleeping and the corks would pop off like gunshots in the house. We would go back there by the tracks on Florida Avenue and we would pick blackberries and she would make blackberry dumplings. It was the blackberries, you cook them and she would take pieces of dough and drop into the berries and let the dumplings cook with the berries. It was blackberry dumplings, like people make chicken and dumplings. Sweet. I haven't seen a wild cherry tree in a long time, but the blackberries still grow on the train tracks.

"My wife just cooks. Over the years, she grew into her cooking. She was very young when we got married, sixteen or something. At the time, I was living across the street from my mama and I would tell her, 'Look, if you don't know how to do this, go across the street and ask my mama, ask my sister, ask my cousin.' But she didn't have to ask nobody. She just cooks. Like a drummer that enjoys their own music? That's how she is with her cooking. She enjoys her own cooking. Asking her to cook is trouble. I just take it as it comes. When she's not in the mood to cook, she's not going to cook. But when she has that feeling she cooks and she might cook four or five dishes. So I just peep and stay out the way. I've been in the battle for thirty-five years."

—*As told by Ronald Lewis*

Tupelo Street Barbecue

Ronald was very adamant about the name for this recipe, that it be named after the street where he lives: "Because Tupelo Street, wings, and sausage is my domain." You can use any kind of meat with this sauce. Ronald sometimes likes to barbecue thin-cut pork chops. He uses good-quality coals that stay hot for a long time. Another trick he has is to intermittently spray his rack with cooking spray so the meats don't stick.

Serves 10

30 chicken wings
3 pounds Double D smoked sausage
Several shakes Tony Chachere's Creole Seasoning
Several shakes garlic powder
Extra salt and black pepper

Sauce:
1 bottle Kraft Hickory Smoke Onion Bits Barbecue Sauce
1 bottle Kraft Honey Mustard Barbecue Sauce
½ cup honey
Many shakes Tabasco sauce
Juice of 1 lemon
Cayenne to taste

Clean your raw meats under cold, running water. Then season them with the dry seasonings, cover with plastic wrap, and let sit in the refrigerator for a couple of hours. Light your grill and prepare your sauce by just mixing all the ingredients together in a bowl. Grill meats until clear juice comes out when you poke them—they should be almost done. Then start adding sauce with a brush, about 2 layers on each side, turning meats until fully cooked, closing the cover and waiting a few minutes between each basting. Enjoy in the company of friends, family, and neighbors.

Meat Sauce with Dried Shrimp

Ronald does not add thyme, oregano, or basil to his sauce because that's how he remembers his mother doing it. But he also wants to remind you to cook to your own taste, adding whatever you like.

Serves 12

3 pounds ground chuck
1 ounce dried shrimp
2 tablespoons oil
1 green bell pepper, diced
2 yellow onions, diced
2–3 ribs celery, sliced
2–3 green onions, chopped
1 (6-ounce) can tomato paste
1 (29-ounce) can tomato sauce
1 (28-ounce) can whole tomatoes
2 bay leaves
1 tablespoon dried parsley
Tony Chachere's Creole Seasoning
Salt and black pepper

Heat the oil in a large pot and sauté the bell pepper, yellow onion, celery, and green onions for a few minutes over medium heat to "get the flavor going in the pot." Add meat, separating and browning it. Add tomato paste, spreading it over everything in the pot. Add tomato sauce, whole tomatoes, dried shrimp, bay leaf, and parsley. Simmer and stir for a couple of hours, adding Tony's, salt, and pepper to taste. Serve with pasta and plenty of Parmesan cheese.

Arthur "Okra" Robinson

Have You Seen the Fruit Man?

New Orleans once had more public markets than any other American city, bringing local specialties and fresh produce to almost every neighborhood. The market was a favorite hangout, gathering neighbors from next door and from the block over. The city had built as many as thirty-four municipal markets by 1911. Many of them were renovated or rebuilt during the 1930s only to then be sold off. Large-scale privatization into the late 1940s, when Mayor deLesseps Story Morrison was in office, was supposed to improve sanitation and food quality, but many of the public market buildings soon hosted other types of businesses. During the first years of Morrison's administration, the number of streetcar lines was also reduced from twelve—including the famous Desire line—to only two, Canal and St. Charles, many being replaced by buses. People could now drive to new, private supermarkets that had modern refrigeration and were outside the center of the city. All the while, local fruit and vegetable men have bought up surplus produce and taken it into the neighborhoods. Fruit and vegetable man Arthur "Okra" Robinson continues to drive his truck all over Downtown. His father, "Okra," was a fruit and vegetable man, and his brother, "Okra," was a fruit and vegetable man too. Many recognize Arthur Robinson's song, "I've got oranges and bananas, I have eating pears and apples, I have grape, cantaloupe, I have plum, I have nectarine, I have okras, I have cabbage, sweet potatoes, orange potatoes, I have onion, I have garlic," as he drives up and down the streets.

A Blood Pull

"There are fruitful days, and unfruitful days. I try to plant by the moon."

BERTIN ESTEVES TURNS TO SPAIN AND THE FAMILY FARM FOR INSPIRATION: "The Isleños came here as militiamen. My family arrived 1779. They came from La Gomera, one of the seven islands of the Canaries. Our people brought with them their traditions, their cooking habits and remedies.

"My mother, who learned from the family, was of Irish descent. My mother was a good cook, and I think she learned it from my father's mother, who was Creole. My father spoke Creole, Spanish Creole. My mother did most of the cooking. She was a regular housewife. We had a great big yard and we always had a garden, and that's what he added to it, I think.

"I learned to cook by making mistakes. I look at other people's recipes, but I don't necessarily follow them. I take what I like and add what I like. I guess I experimented on my children when they were young. Seriously, I became more interested in cooking after my first trip to Spain in 1966. I was cooking Spanish food before that and I had paella in Madrid and said, 'I cook better paella!' We eat a lot of rice here. Rice, it's hard to go wrong with rice. I make a rice sandwich. You cook some rice and mince up some onions or peppers or something and mayonnaise and put that on bread.

Bertin Bernard Esteves, Jr.

BORN
1931 in New Orleans, Louisiana

LIVES IN
St. Bernard

OCCUPATION
Tour guide

HOLY TRINITY
Red onion, green bell pepper, garlic

WHY NOT?
Raccoon for Christmas

"Now my interest is tapas. There are so many things you can do with tapas, dates and goat cheese, bananas wrapped with bacon. That's very simple, very common. I also do sliced oranges cooked down in sugar water; it's a sweet tapa. We call them appetizers, but in Spain it's a tradition, when they get off work at night, they usually parade to a couple of tapas bars and drink some wine. Tapas can be almost anything bite-size, so to speak. Finger food.

"I got my first recipe for caldo from a black woman who used to work in the French Quarter. It was a bean soup, very

Bertin Esteves spends most of his time among his brother's citrus trees. He lived in a trailer before Katrina, and still does today.

similar to our caldos. We use a lot of white beans in them, potatoes, turnip greens, everything. It's like a stew. I asked her for her recipe, and then I realized how similar it was.

"What I ate as a child is now being called soul food. Red beans and rice, chicken stew, or pork chop. My mother, not knowing why, was very conscious of bugs on lettuce, and she would cook pork chops so hard you could wear them on the bottom of your shoes. We ate a lot of rice, a lot of beans. Probably a lot of fat.

"My grandfather grew wild cherry trees. From him, my father learned how to make the cherry bounce. And I make the cherry bounce. It's a little purple cherry; they don't get any bigger than a green pea. I ferment them with sugar for six months. Then you mix alcohol with it, and then you can strain it. I rework my cherries. As soon as I've drained them and bottled the liquid, I add sugar to the old cherries, or I'll split the old mother and add new cherries. I've got cherries I've been working for three or four years now, adding a little bit at a time. You get less and less production out of them, but they're still good. And they're sour

cherries. If you eat them, you're going to spit them out. But you ferment them with sugar and it's unbelievable the transition the cherry makes.

"The farm, we inherited it. My brother raised a family on it. When my father died I sold my share to my brother. But now that I'm retired, I'm always there. I guess it's a blood pull or something; I enjoy myself just sitting there at the farm. I enjoy working with him. I think it's made us like brothers should be.

"My father didn't farm until he retired. He worked for a sugar refinery. And his father farmed, and his father's father. Actually, I'm still learning. I'm learning from my brother how to

Rice Rules

Jambalaya might be the Isleños's largest contribution to the Louisiana table, but the lineages of local dishes are about as impossible to trace as New Orleans family trees. The Isleños are Canary Islanders who were sent here by King Juan Carlos III of Spain to protect New Orleans from the British during the American Revolution. Spanish influence on jambalaya is certain. Jambalaya, with its rich mix of meats, rice, and spice, is clearly related to paella. But composed rice dishes are common

all over West Africa as well. Louisiana jambalaya was probably born from many different influences. Tee Wayne Abshire, a regular contender in the World Jambalaya Championship in Gonzales, says Louisiana jambalaya has not changed since the competition started in the 1960s: "I cook the same jambalaya every time, the one I cook at home. Eventually you find the right set of judges."

Isleño Home Remedies

Bertin's friend Cecile Jones Robin has documented many of the Isleño community's home remedies. Some of them are: lemon to remove a tan; turnips to cure laryngitis; garlic for athlete's foot; onions for burns; warm salt in a sock on the belly to cure

colic; celery to relieve rheumatism; beets to pass kidney stones; basil tea for headaches; potato under the foot for fevers; coffee for asthma; and figs for constipation.

graft fruit trees now. From my uncle I learned how far apart you space the rows.

"Our people came from the Canary Islands, which is mountainous. And they came to a land that's below sea level, and they adapted what they could find here. Spain did give them provisions and everything to plant, so they could grow the foods they were used to. That's how caldo comes down to us and other things. I think, out of respect for our ancestors, we should try and preserve. Something."

—As told by Bertin Esteves

Pecan Tapas

This is a spicy snack for nibbling fingers. Make sure you get plenty to drink!

1 pound pecan halves
2 tablespoons vegetable oil
1 teaspoon salt
1 teaspoon cayenne
1 teaspoon black pepper
1 teaspoon oregano and/or thyme
⅓ cup honey, or honey and syrup mixed

In a heavy skillet, heat oil over medium heat. Add spices, then honey. Stir and simmer over low heat for a few minutes. You are trying to get rid of some of the water in the honey but not cook it so much that it will clump instead of coat pecans. Add pecans, coating well. Transfer pecans to an oiled cookie sheet and bake in the oven at 300 degrees for 15–20 minutes until darker, reddish brown. Stir pecans while they cool, or they will cling to each other and the cookie sheet.

Galician Soup (Caldo Gallego)

Bertin acquired this recipe on a trip to Spain, but it's a lot like the soul food he grew up eating.

Serves 6–8

1 cup dried white beans
3 quarts water
1-pound flank steak, cut into large pieces (see directions)
½-pound ham hock
2-ounce piece salt pork, without rind
1 green bell pepper, chopped
1 onion, chopped
1 teaspoon salt
3 chorizos or any spicy sausage
2 large potatoes, peeled and diced
½ pound turnip greens, shredded (remove stems)
Black pepper to taste

Rinse beans and soak overnight in water to cover. Drain and place in a stockpot with water, steak, ham hock, salt pork, bell pepper, onion, and salt. Bring to a boil, reduce heat to low and simmer, covered, for 1½ hours. Add sausage, potatoes, and turnip greens. Continue to simmer on low until beans are tender, about 30 minutes. Remove ham hock, cut meat off bone, and return meat to pot. Remove flank steak, shred it finely with a fork, and return to pot. Discard salt pork. Season to taste and serve in warmed bowls, over rice or alone.

Satsumas with Sangria Syrup

Yesterday's wine put to good use! This syrup is delicious over any type of fresh fruit salad. You can also use it as a glaze for pork roast, to which you can add chunks of fresh garlic, rosemary, and caramelized onion. "If you read Spanish cookbooks, you'll find that they use a lot of citrus in their recipes. I've used satsumas when a Spanish recipe calls for oranges, because they're easy to peel, easier to segment." (Author's note: You can add the peel of half an orange or a teaspoon of cardamom seeds or whole cloves at the beginning and let this simmer with the syrup for more flavor. Just remember to strain the syrup after it cools.)

Makes ½ cup

1 cup red wine
½ cup sugar

Bring ingredients to a low boil and simmer for 15–20 minutes until syrup has reduced to about half and coats the back of a spoon. Cool.

Popeye's on a Plane

*"Beans for breakfast, beans for lunch,
beans for dinner. I like beans."*

—Maria Altagracia Garcia

MARIA, DOLORES, AND MARIA GARCIA KNOW THE TASTE OF HOME:

BIG MARIA: "Red beans and rice is a different color in Honduras. It's called casamiento, marriage. Marriage for beans and rice. But it's also called moros y christianos, gallo pinto, or just rice and beans."

DOLORES: "It depends on the way you prepare it, on your race. On the north coast where we are Garifunas, we call it moros y christianos. That means Moors and Christians. There's also another culture, called the Miskito, and that's Garifuna, Indian and European together, and they call it gallo pinto, going more towards Salvador, and they put tomatoes and other things. But we do beans and rice and coconut milk."

BIG MARIA: "It's a different taste."

DOLORES: "We make our own coconut milk from scratch. You grate the fresh coconut meat and mix it with hot water. Let it sit, and then you start squeezing the coconut to get the oil out."

BIG MARIA: "I came to New Orleans in August of 1970, and then we went back to Honduras in 1982 so that my children could go to school there. It's coming here and going and coming back. My husband was on a ship, gone for six months, nine months, all the time. And then I had the accident."

DOLORES: "She got shot in Honduras."

BIG MARIA: "Six shots in my back. But God is beautiful. I am still here. God is beautiful."

DOLORES: "That was 1994."

BIG MARIA: "It was my nephew. Maybe it was drugs, I don't know. I was going to church, going from my house. Bang, bang, bang. So now my husband has become a cook. I tell him, put onion, put this, and it's good cooking. He makes everything and it's taste good. Sometimes I miss my mama, and I tell him I'd like to eat something, and he makes it. Sopa de albondigas, meatball soup, with plantains and eggs. I like it. Pork and rice soup. Or capirotadas, corn and cheese dumplings, you fry them and put them in soup with onion,

Left

Dolores Altagracia Garcia

BORN
1976 in New Orleans, Louisiana

NEIGHBORHOOD
Irish Channel

OCCUPATION
Paralegal

HOLY TRINITY
Onion, cumin, tomato

DREAM JOB?
Lawyer, with a bakery on the side!

Center

Maria Altagracia Garcia

BORN
1950 in Trujillo, Honduras

NEIGHBORHOOD
Irish Channel

OCCUPATION
Housewife (grandmother)

HOLY TRINITY
Salt, cumin, garlic

THE DAUGHTERS' COOKING?
"It's good, but . . ."

Right

Maria Tomasa Garcia

BORN
1971 in New Orleans, Louisiana

NEIGHBORHOOD
Irish Channel

OCCUPATION
Administrative assistant (life insurance)

HOLY TRINITY
Onion, bell pepper, tomato

WEEKLY MENU?
Cooks the same dish, again and again and again!

Oscarito Garcia waits for the piñata to drop at his birthday party. In the background, from left to right: Mohammad Salehpour; Dolores, Marcelino, Maria, Maria, and Oscar Garcia; Marshanique Stevenson; Dolores's husband, Cesar Zelaya, with their daughter, Sophia, on his shoulders.

pepper, celery, and cilantro. You like it potatoes? You like it bananas? You like it yuca? You put it inside."

DOLORES: "She likes to bake breads too. She makes all kinds of sweet and simple breads. She loves to make bread and I love to eat the bread she makes."

BIG MARIA: "Cemitas, pan dulce, coconut bread, sweet potato bread, yuca bread, banana bread, quesadillas. Different, different, different. Torta, cake, I make it too. I make pie, I make donuts, I make everything. My grandmother and my mother baked, I looking and tried. When we married, I no cook. I know nothing. When I see my husband and he no cook, open the can and put it on the fire? I don't like it, so I cooked. I call my mama, I call my friend. What do you put? What do you do?"

LITTLE MARIA: "All our recipes are in my mom's mind. I flake all the time and forget one or two ingredients. I was telling

"There are so many Hondurans in New Orleans it's like leaving Honduras and coming to Honduras in another place."

—Dolores Altagracia Garcia

Dolores, we have to write these things down, and we never do. We just go, 'Mom, what do I put in it?'"

DOLORES: "We grew up in Trujillo, the first founded city in Honduras. That's where Christopher Columbus did his first mass when he came to America, in front of the beach. In Trujillo, you wouldn't find that much vegetables. You would

—Maria Tomasa Garcia

only find potatoes, carrots, cabbage, bananas, platinums [plantains]. What else? Chayote, the mirliton. You won't see broccoli or cauliflower over there; it's just the basics. People eat sopa de caracol, conch soup, like a sea snail, there was even a song about it; it's typical from there."

BIG MARIA: "We make jambalaya in Honduras too. It's different, because we put chorizo."

DOLORES: "We missed New Orleans food when we lived in Honduras, especially fast food. They don't have McDonald's in Trujillo. They don't have Pizza Hut in Trujillo. They don't have Dunkin' Donuts. They don't have Popeye's."

BIG MARIA: "But I made it in the house."

DOLORES AND LITTLE MARIA: "But it's not the same!"

LITTLE MARIA: "When Mom would travel from New Orleans, we always made her bring us Popeye's on the plane. She would bring us Popeye's to Trujillo."

DOLORES: "People on the plane would complain because it has a strong smell."

LITTLE MARIA: "We missed beignets. When I came here, the first thing I wanted to do was go eat Popeye's, eat crawfish, and eat beignets. That's what I wanted to do, as soon as I got home. My mama's donuts are good and everything, but it's different and it's these things you miss."

DOLORES: "In crawfish season, we eat three pounds each every week. So we eat a lot of crawfish. We start in late January,

and now it's June and we're still eating some. Until they say at the store, 'No more crawfish!'"

LITTLE MARIA: "Everything we've learned, we've learned from our mom. We call her. I celebrated Thanksgiving in Honduras, and my mom was here and she didn't want us to lose our American customs so we celebrated Thanksgiving and Independence Day in Honduras. She wouldn't let us forget where we came from. My parents were good at that; they did not let us forget our American history. I was over there for so long and I just wanted to come home. For me, this is home. New Orleans is home."

BIG MARIA: "My children born here. Me was born in Honduras. It's two cultures. It's good."

—As told by Maria, Dolores, and Maria Garcia

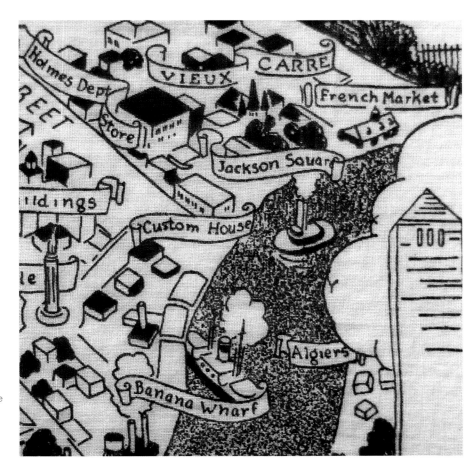

Detail from an old New Orleans scarf with a city map, showing the location of the banana wharf.

Bananas for New Orleans

New Orleans hosts about ten thousand Hondurans, according to census data. Many arrived in the 1960s, first settling in the Lower Garden District and Irish Channel area and then moving into suburbs like Kenner. Fruit is at the center of this immigrant story. There was a New Orleans family from Sicily named Vaccaro who made money by selling produce. They started thinking about how they could earn more. What about coconuts? Or better, bananas? The Vaccaros eventually established the Standard Fruit Company, shipping bananas from Honduras to the United States through New Orleans, which the United Fruit Company also did. Standard Fruit eventually owned and operated many ships, sailing between New Orleans and La Ceiba in Honduras, but also stopping in Havana and other ports. The banana connection explains in part why so many Hondurans today live in New Orleans. Honduras and other Central American countries became known as "banana republics" because of the power and influence of the fruit companies there.

Seafood Soup (Sopa Marinera)

Big Mama says, "The most important thing is you chop and chop and chop. Your onions, your pepper, your celery; it gives you gravy. If you chop big, not give you the gravy." If you decide to use conch, tenderize the meat by pounding it with a mallet before you put it in the soup.

Serves 8

1 tomato, diced
1 small onion, diced
1 rib celery, diced
1 green bell pepper, diced
2 cloves garlic, minced
2 tablespoons olive oil
2 tablespoons flour
2 teaspoons red achiote (annatto) oil or enough for color
1 (14-ounce) can coconut milk
3 cans (use coconut milk can) water
2 pounds yuca, yam, malanga (cocoyam), plantains or green
    bananas of your choice, peeled and cut into large chunks
½ teaspoon cumin
2 teaspoons salt
½ teaspoon black pepper
Cayenne (optional)
2 pounds fish, gumbo crabs, shrimp, and/or conch meat

Sauté tomato, onion, celery, bell pepper, and garlic in olive oil. Stir in flour and achiote. Add coconut milk and water, a little at a time, to make a smooth soup base. Bring to a boil. Add starches and simmer, covered, for 20 minutes. Season soup with cumin, salt, black pepper, and cayenne. Add seafood. Bring back to a boil and simmer, covered, for 10 minutes. Serve.

"Gunned Down" or "Hacked with a Machete" (Baleadas or Machetadas)

These are two of the most common street foods in Honduras. Baleadas and machetadas are basically the same dish, but served differently. Baleadas means "gunned down" and is a wrap made with a flour tortilla cooked in a dry, hot skillet until dark brown or black circles appear on the bread. Machetadas means "hacked with a machete," which refers to how the tortilla dough is cut before it is deep-fried. Another popular street treat is hojaldra, similar to beignets. Dolores makes these from the same dough. She shapes them like tortillas but makes them as thin as possible. She then deep-fries them and serves them with colored syrup. You can make the syrup by simmering 1 cup of sugar, 1 cup of water, and red or blue food coloring together until it coats the back of a spoon (the cooled syrup should be the consistency of maple syrup). Drizzle syrup over fried breads.

Makes 12 breads

For tortillas:

3 cups flour

1 teaspoon salt

1 teaspoon baking powder

1 tablespoon sugar (optional, but recommended by Big Maria)

½ cup vegetable oil

1 egg

1 cup water

Vegetable oil for deep-frying (for machetadas only)

For serving:

Refried or regular cooked beans (preferably small red beans)

Fresh, creamy butter (mantequilla) and/or Latin American white cheese (queso fresco)

Scrambled eggs (cooked with a dash of salt and cumin)

Avocado slices

Make the tortillas by mixing the dry ingredients together and then adding oil, egg, and water. Knead the dough for a few minutes until smooth. Form 12 balls. With floured hands, flatten balls into large rounds. For baleadas, make them as thin as you can. Heat a cast-iron skillet and cook each baleada over medium heat until brown circles appear, turning the baleada once (Dolores says that turning the baleada with your bare hands is a sign of being a "real woman" in Honduras, but it's okay to use implements). For machetadas, cut 4–5 parallel slits in each flattened bread and deep-fry breads one at a time until golden. To serve, dress your baleada with beans and everything else, fold in half, and eat like a wrap. You serve machetadas by putting bread and other items in separate piles on a plate.

On Another Island

*"I have dreams of doing a
baklava assortment equivalent
to a box of chocolates."*

Karen Michael Kyame Clark

BORN
1957 in New Orleans, Louisiana

NEIGHBORHOOD
Gentilly

OCCUPATION
Textile conservator

HOLY TRINITY
Cinnamon, tomato, onion

FAST FOOD?
Creole tomato sandwich
("It tastes better when you
eat it over the sink")

KAREN CLARK'S MOTHER LEFT THE AEGEAN AND FOUND A NEW GREEK ISLAND IN NEW ORLEANS: "My mother's family came from Límnos. She came to New Orleans in the early 1920s, met my father, and stayed here. My sister, my brother, and I were brought up American, but we had Greek food. My mom was around only Greeks. I never ate gumbo or jambalaya until I was in my twenties. I didn't even realize that whole facet, which is kind of fascinating, that I would be oblivious to it. We were like in our own little subculture within the city.

"I was asking my sister, had we really never eaten New Orleans foods growing up? Creole cream cheese is about the only thing I can think of except for red beans. They'd get a container of that and divide it up between all five of us. Creole cream cheese with granulated sugar and strawberries on Sundays after church.

"Sunday afternoons we visited this wonderful lady out in Lakeview who needed help having letters read and bills paid, my mother would translate for her. Visiting Greeks, when we walked into every house, first thing, we would be given this little dish that had this little spoon of preserves on it and a glass of water. My mother said, 'You have to eat the preserves first and then drink the water. Don't stick the preserves in the water.' This is a true Greek tradi-

Karen and her husband, Terry, serve rose petal spoon sweets to guests outside their FEMA trailer, where they were still living almost two years after Katrina, waiting for their egg cream–colored modular home to be finished.

tion to give a spoon sweet. When you come into a house, you're always fed something. My mother would preserve orange rind and have some around the house. There is one lady, invariably, every time I go to her house, whether I'd just eaten or I'm just about to go eat, she's going to make me sit down and eat a meal with her. She is quintessential of what Greek women are like. Cooking, children, church. That's it.

"I cook for the Greek Orthodox church on Robert E. Lee. I bake the bread for the communion and memorial wheat. Catholics, I don't think they do that. When I think of Catholics I think of 'We're having a spaghetti benefit' or 'We're having a fish fry,' and that's not actually part of the church service.

"Being Orthodox, we fasted a lot. If one adds up all of the days we should be fasting it would be roughly half of the year, so we ate shrimp and oysters and crab but not in the way most New Orleanians would prepare it. Stuffed cabbage, stuffed tomatoes, and stuffed bell peppers, that's New Orleanian too, but we didn't have them spiced or seasoned in the New Orleans way, it was spiced or seasoned more in a Greek way. Oregano, cinnamon, cloves, those three spices right there. My mother was really strict about fasting. But there's a fine line with it, it's not so much being that strict, because then you're playing yet another game, you're being coy and righteous about it. If you were going to visit, depending on the situation, if they offered me ice cream on a fast day, in keeping with it one would probably just quietly sit there and eat the ice cream. That might be just as good as fasting, if you're doing it not to create a scene. Fasting is not always so much what you put in your mouth but also what comes out of your mouth, how you treat people. The food is yet another way of being more aware.

"I'm a vegetarian, but I can cook a mean leg of lamb. You put oregano and lemon juice and salt and pepper and butter, slice the potatoes in big wedges, and you roast that. That's the quintessential way of cooking lamb for the Greeks. It's amazing how I did eat in Greece and how I didn't gain weight. I had spinach pies and cheese pies and all these things, if you eat them here in the city and don't walk as much as you did in Greece, you gain weight in a heartbeat. Salads were wonderful there. Food in Greece is very simple, mainly vegetables, cheeses. Life is very laid back. I can understand why many Greeks would find New Orleans a good place to live. We're not in a hurry here.

"I was lucky to be able to go to Greece and study iconography for a little while. And it was funny how, when I got there, I felt at home. I was going, 'This is what Mom was talking about,' and, 'That is what Mom was talking about.' Everything she was telling me about life as a Greek was quite evident there. As one of my friends put it, it's like getting plugged into an electrical socket. You light up.

"One thing in Greece that stood out in my mind was the horta, and horta is nothing more than dandelion greens. I think it's boiled and they add olive oil and possibly lemon juice. Just the smell of it at the little restaurants that had their tables outdoors, I just had to stop and eat a bowl full of it. The nearest thing to it here in New Orleans is the dandelion greens all the black maids would be picking off the neutral ground before they'd go home, you know, taking care of people's houses. I'd see them reaching over and I never understood quite why they were picking the dandelions, but now I do. It's quite a treat to eat that.

"The way Katrina has affected things—it's like being on another planet all together. It's like the astronauts up there at the space station, 'I only have a month more, let me do the science experiments I'm supposed to and eat my MRE meal.' Like Rocket Man. We're here in New Orleans but we're not. You'd think cooking would be therapy right now, but it's not substantial enough to feel normal.

"When I ended up in the trailer, I said, 'Let me see how I can cook,' but it's so crowded in there you don't feel like cooking. I feel like I have an Easy-Bake Oven and a little toy sink. I'm anxious to be in a real kitchen. I think I'm going to go crazy once I get into our house and am able to seriously cook.

"Getting ready to move into a new kitchen, I've stocked up on spoon sweets. This is sour cherry, and that's rose petal. Rose petal jelly, I tried making this one time when I was a girl, and my father spent three hours trying to chisel it out of the saucepan because I accidentally cooked it too long. Oh, and this is Turkish coffee, but we're not supposed to say Turkish. *Greek* coffee.

"Food is a good thing to focus on doing well since it's something that happens every day. It won't be perfect, life's never perfect. But at the end of the day you sit down with a meal. Here's heritage, history being passed on in a very organic way, a common way, it's not in the history book, yet it's a part of the whole chain of history and life."

—As told by Karen Clark

Garlic Bread Dip (Skordalia)

Karen makes this dip with pecans, which is a New Orleans take on a Greek favorite. And she is not afraid to double the amount of garlic. Excellent served with bread, vegetables, and fried foods.

6 cloves garlic
½ teaspoon salt
¾ cup pecans
½ cup water
4 English muffins soaked in water and then squeezed dry
1 cup olive oil
½ cup vinegar

In a blender or food processor, run garlic, salt, pecans, and water until smooth. Add bread, olive oil, and vinegar, alternately. Run until smooth.

Greek Lasagna with Cinnamon (Pastichio)

"The wrong kind of people would probably get a butterfly net and try to catch me, but I like a lot of cinnamon. It cuts the acidity of the tomato paste." This recipe does not call for lasagna sheets but for long macaroni. Karen says that some people take the time to lay all the macaroni in a line across the pan, but she usually just dumps them in. This recipe contains a lot of butter—if you wish, you can reduce the amount of butter in the cream sauce to about half. Karen usually whips about 9 eggs into the cream sauce as well, but this is risky business—eggs often curdle—and isn't necessary for taste or texture.

Serves 8

Cream sauce:
3 cups milk
1½ sticks butter
3 tablespoons flour
3 tablespoons cornstarch
⅓ cup water

New Orleans Spoon Sweets

Most New Orleans Greeks have family ties to the island of Chios, where spoon sweets are said to have originated. Spoon sweets are fruits, nuts, vegetables, or flower petals cooked down and preserved in syrup. While Greeks on Chios make spoon sweets with walnuts, pistachios, and mastic, Greeks on the Isle of Orleans use local ingredients: pecans, orange and grapefruit rinds, watermelon rinds, hard cooking pears, figs, cherries, rose petals, baby eggplants, and kumquats. These spoon sweets are usually served to visitors along with heavy-duty coffee and a tall glass of cold water as in Greece. The tradition continues in New Orleans but is not as common today as it was one or two generations ago.

¼ teaspoon ground nutmeg or to taste

Salt and ground white pepper to taste

Meat mixture:

1 onion, chopped

3 tablespoons butter

⅓ cup water

1½ pounds ground lamb, beef, or soy crumble

3 cloves garlic, minced

¼ cup tomato paste

2 teaspoons ground cinnamon

Salt and pepper to taste

Pasta:

12 ounces long macaroni #7

3 eggs

¼ teaspoon ground nutmeg

¼ teaspoon ground cinnamon

½ cup grated Parmesan cheese

For assembly:

1 tablespoon butter

½ cup grated Parmesan cheese

First, make the cream sauce. Melt butter and whisk in flour until smooth. Slowly add milk, a little at a time, whisking away lumps. Dissolve cornstarch in water and add to hot milk. Stir constantly and simmer until sauce thickens. Season sauce with nutmeg, salt, and white pepper to taste. Next, sauté onion in butter. Add water and simmer until onion becomes soft. Add meat, separating it well. Add garlic, tomato paste, and cinnamon. When meat is cooked, add salt and pepper to taste. Cook macaroni separately; drain. Beat eggs with nutmeg and cinnamon and pour over hot pasta, coating well. Sprinkle generously with Parmesan. Grease an oven-safe deep dish with butter. Start with a thin layer of macaroni, then all the meat, and then a thick layer of macaroni. Cover with cream sauce, sealing well. Sprinkle with cheese. Bake at 350 degrees until the top is golden brown, about 40 minutes.

Baklava

Cold syrup can be added to hot pastry, or hot syrup to cold pastry. The two should never be the same temperature, or you'll end up with soggy baklava. This recipe calls for Louisiana pecans, not walnuts.

Makes 1 large baklava, serving about 35

Syrup:

2 cups water

¾ cup sugar

1½ cups honey

1 tablespoon fresh lemon juice

Rind from ¼ lemon

1 cinnamon stick

6 whole cloves

Pastry:

1 pound pecans, finely chopped

½ cup finely cubed candied or dried fruit (such as cherries, pineapple, or ginger)

½ cup sugar

½ teaspoon ground cloves

1 tablespoon ground cinnamon

2 pounds phyllo pastry sheets (defrosted for 30 minutes, if frozen)

1½ pounds unsalted butter

Clean, soft paintbrush with dark bristles (so you notice if one falls out)

Whole cloves for decoration

Start with syrup (if adding cold syrup to hot baklava—otherwise make the pastry first). Bring all ingredients to a boil in a saucepan and simmer until syrup has reduced to about half, about 30 minutes, skimming foam and watching carefully so syrup does not boil over. You can also add the honey toward the end, and the syrup will not foam as much. Remove lemon rind, cinnamon stick, and cloves. Cool. Syrup should pour easily but be almost as thick as Karo. If syrup seems thin, bring it back to a boil and simmer it longer. Melt butter for pastry, but do not stir; let clarified butter separate from watery milk solids, which gather on the surface and bottom of pan. Pour clarified butter into a bowl. In another bowl, combine pecans, fruit, sugar, and spices (this will be your filling). Brush a baking pan that holds either an entire phyllo sheet or half a phyllo sheet with clarified butter. Start layering phyllo dough, staggering sheets if they do not cover the entire pan. If phyllo sheets are 18 inches by 13 inches, use a 9-by-13-inch pan and fold each sheet in half. Brush clarified butter between every layer and fold of phyllo. After 6–10 layers, add one layer of pecan mixture. Continue with about 4 layers of phyllo between every layer of filling until the baklava is at least 1 inch thick but doesn't go over the edges of the baking pan. Aim for 4–6 layers

of filling in total. Finish with 10 layers of phyllo dough. Brush top with butter. Refrigerate pastry until top feels waxy and hard. Cut baklava into squares and then again on one diagonal, for triangles. Push a whole clove into the top of each piece for looks. Bake in the oven at 375 degrees for 30–40 minutes until golden. Pour cold syrup over hot pastry. It will fizzle.

Tastes of Freedom

"I'm spoiled. I was raised by women. I was raised like a king. We were poor, but we had the best cooks in the world."

Jerome Manuel Smith

BORN
1939 in New Orleans, Louisiana

NEIGHBORHOOD
Sixth and Seventh Wards

OCCUPATION
Social worker

HOLY TRINITY
Onion, greens, goat cheese

SANDWICHES?
Keep you going!

JEROME SMITH STOPS FOR A SANDWICH ON THE KING'S HIGHWAY: "When I was a young boy, there was a company off of Barracks and North Peters specializing in produce, and I had occasion to pass that during the summers, daily, going to meet watermelon trucks, either at night when fish was being unloaded, and when the fish or shrimp or whatever seafood would fall to the ground, we were allowed to pick it up and bring it home. Over a period of time, an old Italian man, I picked up his garbage can and put it on the sidewalk. He witnessed me doing that several times, so we started talking, and ultimately he wanted me to have lunch with him. He would send me to a sandwich place, a grocery now still in the French Quarter, to get a muffuletta. So he introduced me to the muffuletta. I was a youngster, maybe ten, eleven years old, something. He said, 'That's not too good for you now. You try, if you want to live long, be strong, try some of this.' He was eating Italian bread where he would pour the olive oil on the bread with slithers of garlic and tomatoes and onions, and he would eat that. Initially, the onions and the garlic was so strong, I didn't welcome it too much. Then, ultimately, I got a taste for it. At least once or twice a week, I still do that. So I have been doing that for over fifty years. I think the attraction was his whole mannerisms and the way he embraced me.

"I would go to another place, before I went to the river, there was a place down on St. Claude and Touro, there was a sandwich shop, they had some German people in there, and they made the potato sandwiches. Basically French fries and bread with pickles, and they sold this for about twenty-five cent. That was another sandwich.

"There was this man, Johnny Castle, and I was doing a little work on the river on the banana wharves, and he would start cooking around ten, eleven o'clock at night. He would cook anything at night, steaks, pork chops, red beans, this, that, and the other, and I was so thin and skinny that he tried to put some meat on me. In fact, his daughter, Oretha Castle Haley, that was one of my schoolmates. So that food had another kind of value, cause they would be preparing me, not only to go work on the river, but also to go and give out leaflets and stuff after I came from working on the river. And then, in jails . . .

"I was a banana carrier, had bananas on my shoulder. Just like you see them folks in the islands, taking them off the boats, putting them on trucks, what have you. All that, to me, was like a drama that I could never ever explain. Something happened to you. Being on that river and all this cooking and all these rituals that would be going on with these powerful men. They didn't have that automation and stuff, so everything was based on your body and determination, and they were seriously hard workers. Some be eating out of pots, like a whole pot of something, others would come in with sandwiches that you couldn't believe a human could eat all that. They had everything out there. All the kind of greens that you could name, beans and chicken and pork chops. For breakfast, they'd have red beans, hot sausage,

pork chops and butter beans, black-eyed peas, collard greens, stew, that'd be their breakfast. And at one point, by some magic stroke, it would be all gone.

"I eat raw onions every day. Anytime I eat eggs it's with raw onions. I like a lot of onion, because that's sort of related to my experiences as a boy, starting out here, you know. Once I was shopping for beads and feathers in New York for the Mardi Gras and I met this great storyteller, a Jewish man, on Thirty-eighth Street. He would ask me things about New Orleans, I would be bragging on certain things about New Orleans foods, so he started saying, 'Hey, you try this.' So he gave me a bagel with some onions on it and little sliverings of salmon. He and I used to tell each other stories over bagels and salmon. I used to tell him, so strange, about the potatoes and bread and pickles, and he introduced me to the kosher pickles, the different kinds of pickles. He would sit there, make a little sandwich, and he was telling me Jewish stories and giving me pickles and onions. Now, down here in New Orleans, where I first was involved with the potato sandwich with the pickles, it was from a German fellow. Then I started relating to that in terms of the conflicts of the world. I had this little relationship with these two histories, and the negatives of the histories never came on the page because I liked both, both situations.

"As a boy, I was not allowed to eat in every house. You had to know something about the family. We could not eat in certain places because the way you handle food is an extension of your person. That was a value that could not be violated. You'd pay a serious price if they'd catch you eating where you weren't supposed to eat. Because if you're not concerned about that, then you're really not concerned about yourself. If you are reckless and eat anywhere, you'll make other negative decisions too. We used to be invited to, when I was in New York, the most elaborate things with international dishes and all I had was a fruit. I didn't know nothing about the people. And then I had this thing about not overeating. I thought, in terms of what our mission was, to stay focused on whatever reason I was at that gathering, I was there because of my involvement in that struggle. If you eat a lot of food, it breaks your concentration.

"In Montgomery, Alabama, the night before the first freedom rides into Jackson, Mississippi, I was preparing myself over a period of time, had just gotten out of jail in New Orleans, in fact I had jumped bond to go join the freedom rides. Dr. King didn't eat. We had grits and biscuits and sausage, but he was just nibbling on toast. Ultimately, some of the older women got him to eat an egg. Made me know I was onto something. That was so encouraging. I was so young.

"When we were in Mississippi, there was a different kind of freshness of foods. They really took care of the so-called freedom fighters, with fresh milk, and they would make something they'd call pan bread, and I used to love to eat that with the molasses. You get spoiled off of country cooking. During the day in our travels, if we weren't arrested or no one was hurt, we'd stop in another place, and they would fix all kind of stews and sweet potatoes made in all kind of combinations. We looked forward to those feasts. You know, after running from town to town and dealing with a lot of situations where life was at stake. Many times they would give us bags, and we'd be on the highway singing freedom songs with cakes and chickens. They took care of us.

"I went to jail a lot of times. It was often. The beatings and the jailings. All of it was the fight for freedom. If not, my mother would have killed me.

"We would visit my grandmother down by the river, on Chartres Street. That was big fun because all that mixture was in there. They had a community, folks that were Filipino, right off of Franklin, up in there. I used to see them do things with pineapple, and they would have all these different fruits. That's where I first saw kiwi. And they had a cassava something they used to make. There was a mixture of nationalities down by the river. In fact, this is where I first had peanut butter sauce. Fellows coming off the ships. Sometime they would have a soup with peanut butter in it. That was a good one too. Peanut butter soup.

French (No, Wait), German (No, Wait)—Vietnamese Bread

French bread accompanies a slew of New Orleans meals, from barbecue shrimp to Creole chicken stew to gumbo to po-boys. Locals speak fondly of its soft, chewy texture and light, crackly crust. New Orleans's signature bread is definitely not your average American white bread. It was always called French in New Orleans, even though Germans mostly baked it. Leidenheimer Baking Company, founded by an immigrant from Deidesheim, remains in operation in Central City. In the last decades, historic bakeries have received competition from new family operations run by Vietnamese. Dong Phuong Oriental Bakery in New Orleans East bakes thousands of banh mi, Vietnamese-style French bread, every day, serving Vietnamese po-boys to fellow countrymen and Americans alike.

"All them aromas. That's what we're missing. We were coming one night, four years ago, 'What's missing, man?' When I was a boy, you'd have all these aromas coming out of them windows and doors. You could smell something coming out of everybody's house. Something died in the neighborhoods, because people are not cooking. You would come through the alleys; the aromas would just knock you out. You don't have this floating on the air. You don't have that. Like empty, like plastic. The children being able to come out the house and walk down the alley, you know the narrow alleys, Miss Alma may be cooking something, getting that flavor in your nose, then you go in your own house and there's another kind of aroma, then you're mixed up, then you come out walk on the streets, and all that's happening."

—As told by Jerome Smith

French Market Creole Tomato Sandwich

This is the sandwich that Jerome learned to make from an old, Italian man near Barracks Street and the river. If the tomato is very ripe, he recommends sticking it in your mouth and sucking some of the juice out of it before you slice it. Jerome remembers the old Italian man running his knife through a fresh lemon from time to time to keep it clean.

Italian, French, or pita bread
Olive oil
Creole tomato, sliced
Red onion, thinly sliced
Garlic, thinly sliced

Pour olive oil over the bread. Add tomato, red onion, and garlic.

Banana Bread

You only need two ingredients for this recipe—banana and bread. Jerome used to make this sandwich a lot as a youngster. He came up with the squeezing method because he didn't want to touch the inside of the banana when his hands were dirty. As a child, he usually ate this on French bread. Today, he prefers pita bread.

1 banana
1 piece of bread

Leave the skin on the banana and cut it in half crosswise. Squeeze the banana out of its skin onto the bread. Fold the bread over the banana and eat.

Town and Country

"I love to cook, but I sure hate to wash up. And when I cook, I can dirty up some pots!"

AVERY BASSICH WAS TAUGHT BY THE BEST: "This is one of my pride and joys. It's a cookbook, hand copied and given to my grandmother when she was married in 1893. The recipes are from this lady Ms. Pritchard who lived down in the Garden District. My family was Anglican so these are like the Virginia to eastern seaboard, colonial recipes. Religion has a great deal to do with things that you eat and you cook. My husband's family is Catholic, and Catholics have more of the Latin, a bit more spice, and if you study recipes you can sort of see where the families came from and how they evolved.

"Supposedly Catholics were not meant to eat any meat during the Lent. But you could eat fish and teal duck. Supposedly they could eat the teal because the archbishop said that the duck was a fish-eating duck. Well, a teal is not a fish-eating duck. I think that the good archbishop with the good Catholics just wanted to eat duck.

"When I had to start cooking ducks, they're a mess! Here comes Beau with the bloody ducks! So I really don't like duck. It's very nouveau riche of me to say that, because it's considered a delicacy. But during World War II we had the food rationing and we ate venison, venison, venison and duck, duck, duck. So don't give me duck unless I have to have it.

Avery McLoughlin Bassich

BORN
1930 in New Orleans, Louisiana

NEIGHBORHOOD
University area

OCCUPATION
Housewife

HOLY TRINITY
Celery, bell pepper, green onion

ALWAYS IN HER PURSE?
Tabasco!

"Things have come to be simple. I cooked turkey the other day in the microwave in a little plastic bag. It was really right good, very moist. I never thought I'd cook a turkey in a microwave. I've cooked them over spits; we've cooked them in the oven. When I was little, I lived in the country on Avery Island, and the old stove was a great big old wood-burning stove, and I used to go into the kitchen, I always loved to watch the black cooks. I don't know how they could control the heat, but they cooked wonderful things, biscuits and rolls. They taught us, and if we were assigned to them that day and they told us to do something, we'd better do it. I guess that's when I learned to love cooking.

"We didn't learn nutrition as much as hygiene. My grandmother had cows. The milk would be brought in and poured into these nice big earthen crocks. And then we would skim it. We made butter and we made cream cheese, they call it Creole cream cheese. And the washing of the utensils, oh God! Because of milk and the bacteria, my aunt, who was really rabid on that, we would wash and wash, and she had these huge pots of boiling water that the women really couldn't handle, they would get the gardener or something. It took twice as long to wash everything as it did to make the cream cheese. But that was cleanliness and hygiene.

"Creole cream cheese, we made wonderful ice cream out of it and several recipes. My daddy loved to put brown sugar on it and fresh fruit and you ate it for breakfast. Strawberries when they were in season. Figs! Fig ice cream, that was something else.

"My great-aunt married someone from Philadelphia. She would come back down to Avery Island in the spring for about six weeks, and she would bring all of her servants, Irish maids, and one thing she absolutely adored was bear fat. Bear! The fat would have to be rendered and cooked and strained and boiled. It smells to high heaven when they're rendering, it's a strong, gagging smell. When it is done right, it is a clear, clear oil. And I promise you; it fries to perfection. And Auntie would go back to Philadelphia with a big jar of bear fat.

"When I cook bacon, I strain and keep the grease. If you're cooking okra and tomatoes it's a cardinal sin if you cook it in anything but bacon grease. I have two jars in the refrigerator.

"Nobody measured much of anything. I have Mother's cookbook upstairs. A piece of butter the size of an egg or a piece of butter the size of a large pecan. Frequently, it was equal amounts of flour and eggs. And the scale, the good old cooks, they'd do this [Avery moves her hands up and down like bowls on a scale], they could sort of dump it in, and it usually was right! That was experience. I asked my mother's cook right before I got married, 'Mandy, how do I know how much salt to put on something?' I said, 'I've watched you and you never measure your salt.' 'Oh, no, ma'am,' she says. 'You go once across the top and halfway back with the salt box, and it always is right, Miss Avery.' And darn if she's not right! Whether it's a little pot or a big pot, we always cooked in iron pots, I still have some of my mother's, but once across the top and halfway back is enough. Usually.

"A lot of those recipes, the black people, that's where all of us, where we really learned cooking. I still feel that the blacks cooked better. I still think they do today. They still have a flair."

—As told by Avery Bassich

Cold Alligator Pear Bisque

This soup is not made from alligator meat and pears but from ripe avocados.

Makes 2 quarts

3 or 4 ripe avocados, pitted and peeled
1 tablespoon lemon juice
1½ cups sour cream
4 cups chicken stock or broth
¼ cup chopped green onion
Salt and Tabasco to taste (start with 4 dashes)

Run all ingredients in a blender until smooth. Refrigerate until thoroughly chilled. Serve in chilled bowls or mugs. Garnish with a dollop of sour cream or salsa. Sprinkle with paprika.

Grillades

Avery says she should be tired of grillades and grits since the dish is so commonplace: "You see grillades and grits at every supper after a ball." But she still loves to eat it. When Avery and her husband, Beauregard, were newlyweds, she used to make grillades out of venison. Her trick for good grillades? "Beat the devil out of the meat!" As for making her roux in the oven, she says, "Lord forbid if my mother could hear me say that."

Serves 8

½ cup browned flour
4–5 pounds veal or beef rounds (veal is best, but more
    expensive)
½ cup flour seasoned with garlic powder, salt, and black pepper
½ cup bacon drippings (from about 8 thick-cut bacon strips)
1 cup chopped yellow onion
1 cup chopped green onion
1 cup chopped celery

Some Like It Hot

Hot sauce is a fixture on New Orleans tables, towering over salt and pepper shakers. Avery Bassich's family comes from Avery Island, home of the world-famous Tabasco pepper sauce and the salt mines where the salt for the sauce comes from. Avery is related through her mother, Louise Avery, to Edmund McIlhenny, who first planted seeds of Mexican Tabasco pep-pers there about 140 years ago. Tabasco pepper sauces compete for spots on local tables with Crystal and Louisiana hot sauces. Of these three brands, Langenstein's Supermarket on Arabella (the street where Avery lives) sells about 45 percent Tabasco, 40 percent Crystal, and 15 percent Louisiana.

1 cup chopped green bell pepper

2 cloves garlic, minced

1 cup beef stock

1 (28-ounce) can whole tomatoes

1 pinch of sugar

2–3 bay leaves

1 teaspoon thyme

Salt to taste

½ teaspoon black pepper

Tabasco sauce to taste

1 cup red wine (optional)

½ cup chopped parsley

Brown flour ahead of time by roasting it, dry, in a cast-iron pan in the oven at 400 degrees for about 1½ hours, stirring often, until flour is cinnamon brown. Cool. You can brown more than you need for this recipe and keep it in a sealed container for months. Between two sheets of parchment paper, pound meat. Cut out fat (if any) and cut into strips. Dredge meat in seasoned flour and brown in about half the grease in an iron pot. As meat browns, remove and drain on paper bags. In a Dutch oven, sauté onion, green onion, celery, bell pepper, and garlic in remaining grease. Stir in browned flour and mix thoroughly. Add beef stock and stir until it thickens. Add tomatoes, sugar, bay leaves, and thyme. Mix well and cook for several minutes over low heat, mashing tomatoes. Add meat and stir well. Taste before adding salt, pepper, and Tabasco. Cover pot and cook over low heat at least 1 hour. Stir occasionally to prevent sticking. Grillades should be tender enough to cut with a fork. Veal will be tender in less time than beef. Allow dish to sit for several hours, or refrigerate overnight. Reheat before serving and add wine. Garnish with parsley and serve with cheese grits.

Hungary for Figs

"Hypertension, diabetes, that's my bread and butter."

—Stephen Gergatz

STEPHEN GERGATZ AND JULIANNA BIKA LOOK FOR FIG TREES WHEREVER THEY GO:

STEPHEN: "New Orleans is figs."

JULIANNA: "For us, fig is very unique. Because in Hungary, we don't have this. If you go to Croatia, the sea, for vacation, then we have figs but it was such a big deal for us. Because in Hungary, we never saw figs. Only when we went to Yugoslavia. Maybe Bulgaria had some figs. That's the places we could only travel. There is figs in Italy, but you could not travel to Italy, because we were a Socialist country and you could not go. Just every third year, and you had to have a lot of money to go to Italy so

Stephen Joseph Gergatz	Julianna Bika
BORN 1946 in Lövő, Hungary	**BORN** 1951 in Budapest, Hungary
NEIGHBORHOOD Uptown (West End pre-Katrina)	**NEIGHBORHOOD** Uptown (West End pre-Katrina)
OCCUPATION Doctor of internal medicine	**OCCUPATION** Accountant, journalist
HOLY TRINITY Paprika, onion, garlic	**HOLY TRINITY** Paprika, onion, garlic
GUMBO? Goulash!	**MOTHER MADE?** Doberge cake!

Drinking coffee is a big part of the couple's daily routine. They start with coffee at home with breakfast, and then the local coffee shops might see them two or three times in one day.

you could not travel to Italy but you could go to Yugoslavia. That place I remember that we could have figs. Figs, it was a vacation, so everybody in Hungary has this certain image about figs."

STEPHEN: "My wife gave me, because I love them, a collection of sixty recipes using fresh figs."

JULIANNA: "That was Christmas in 1992. I searched in cookbooks. It was difficult to find the recipes, maybe one or two on the Internet."

STEPHEN: "Once a year we have a fig meal. Every course is figs. Lots of people have them in their yards. We get them from neighbors, friends. We know who has figs. I have patients who have fig trees. We talk about food. If you're constipated, you can take figs. 'I can't move my bowels.' 'Why don't you eat fresh figs?' 'Oh, I've got a fig tree in my backyard.' 'Can

I pick some?' I go out to their home and pick figs. In a two-week period they all become ripe. You could have the whole city pick and there still would be figs on the trees."

JULIANNA: "We went to Mr. Gubert in River Ridge, and he had a very small house but he had a big garage, and we stood on the top of his garage and were collecting the figs on the fig trees."

STEPHEN: "Fig season is around the beginning of July. The trees are getting ready so I'm getting ready. We're going to make fig mousse, peeled figs that you put in the blender with whipping cream and sugar, that's one way of making it. You can also make jams using figs and strawberry gelatin, and it tastes exactly like strawberries. Hungarians are in the history of the strawberry farming. You know, this is the strawberry belt. Italians started it and Hungarians learned it from the

Italians. We eat a lot of strawberries here. More than we ate in Hungary. I had strawberries for breakfast, grits and strawberries and coffee. I often have grits, a real New Orleans breakfast. I usually put blueberries in the grits, but today I used strawberries."

JULIANNA: "We don't throw away food. When we were younger we didn't throw away any food, tried to. My husband is a gastroenterologist, so we know when it's spoiled. In his childhood, with his parents, they had this internment; they had to go to the country for a couple of years. Because they weren't politically correct or something, they were sent where was no running water, no food, nothing. So we never throw away food. It's a bad feeling. Especially what you make, what you buy, it's a lot of work, you do it with love and then you forget it in the Frigidaire. Oh, I feel so guilty. We are not religious but my husband is Catholic and I learned it from the Catholics that if you throw away bread, then, I don't know, Jesus is crying. It's always in my head, even if I'm not religious. In my childhood, I was always hungry. Our sweet was the bread with the lard and then sugar on top. That was the sweet. You never put something else on the bread. That was my grandmother. Either butter or cheese; you don't put two stuffs, like sandwich. No! There is something on your bread, that's enough. Butter and cheese? That'd be too extravagant!"

STEPHEN: "There's an interesting story about the doberge cake. Doberge cake was created by a Hungarian chef named Joseph Dobos in the late 1800s. It requires a hard caramel layer on the top, but for some reason because of climate, that didn't work here. So they switched to a ganache top. They started pronouncing dobos *d'auberge*, 'of the inn,' as if this is a French cake. Like cake this good has to be French. I had a

"I think it's good for you to be hungry a little bit and work for your food."

—Julianna Bika

food critic for *Gourmet* magazine come down and he wanted to research the exact lineage of the dobos to doberge. And he could not do it. He could not find the trail. You have to look in private journals, diaries. I've had it in Hungary and I've had New Orleans doberge also. They're different. Hungarian comes in one flavor, chocolate. Americans make it lemon and chocolate. There's no such thing in Hungary, lemon doberge. There's no lemons. But we have cracklings in Hungary, like here."

JULIANNA: "In Hungary when you have a party, you start it with hot goose cracklings. It has to be goose. And Slivowitz, the plum brandy. That is when the big party starts."

STEPHEN: "Cajun cracklings is the pork rinds that are cooked down in lard, and this is very common in Hungary too. Hungarians in New Orleans buy cracklings from the Cajuns and make crackling biscuits. You chop them up and bake them into little breads, and you have them in the morning or afternoon."

JULIANNA: "When I was a student in Hungary and I loved dresses, I used to eat only cracklings because that was the cheapest food. I was so amazed, in the Cajun country, when I first saw, 'What? I'm coming to America to eat cracklings?' People standing in line for cracklings?! I never forget that."

—As told by Stephen Gergatz and Julianna Bika

Cold Melon Mint Soup

This is Julianna's favorite summer soup.

Serves 4

1 English cucumber, peeled and cut into 1-inch pieces
2 cups honeydew melon pieces (about 1½ pounds)
1 cup plain yoghurt
¼ cup fresh mint leaves (about 24 leaves)
2 tablespoons (or more) fresh lime juice
Salt to taste (about 1 teaspoon)
White pepper to taste (about ½ teaspoon)
Mint leaves for garnish

Combine cucumber, honeydew, yoghurt, mint, and lime juice in a bowl and puree in batches in a blender. Pour mixture through a sieve, and season with salt and pepper. Chill, covered, for at least 2 hours. Serve soup garnished with mint.

Fried Bread (Lángos)

Julianna calls this her "Lakeview recipe," as the couple lived in Lakeview, minutes from Dorignac's supermarket, before Hurricane Katrina. Lángos are savory snacks and can be served with pretty much anything. They're like savory beignets.

French bread dough
Peanut oil for frying
Salt
Sour cream

Call Dorignac's supermarket the day before and ask them to set aside French bread dough the next morning. Buy dough. Take dough and make flat rounds, about 6 inches in diameter and half an inch (or less) thick. Drop dough into hot oil and deep-fry until golden brown on both sides, puncturing holes with a fork at the beginning. Drain on paper towels and sprinkle with salt. Eat warm with sour cream.

Duck with Fresh Figs

If you've never cooked duck before, this is an easy way to start. You will probably have about a cup of duck fat left over after you've made this. Don't throw the duck fat away; save it for another recipe, like white beans.

Serves 2–4

4-pound duckling
2 dozen fresh figs
2 cups port wine
Salt and pepper
2 tablespoons butter
2 tablespoons brandy

Wash figs, remove hard part of stems, and soak in wine in a covered jar for 24 hours. Wash duck and wipe dry. Sprinkle with salt and pepper. Place duck in a casserole pan with butter. Bake, uncovered, at 325 degrees for about 30 minutes. Drain off fat. Add the marinating wine, reserving the figs. Return duck to oven and continue cooking for 1 hour or until duck is tender, basting occasionally with wine. Skim off fat. Add figs and cook for 10 more minutes. Transfer duck to a warmed platter and place figs around it. Add brandy to pan drippings, heat, season with salt and pepper, and spoon some sauce over duck. Serve remaining sauce in a sauceboat. Serve with rice and green beans or peas.

Feed Me, Guide Me

*"I make good Buffalo wings.
I say it's my old grandfather's recipe,
but I just made it up."*

Asare Dankwah

BORN
1959 in Kumasi, Ghana

NEIGHBORHOOD
Central City

OCCUPATION
Clergy

HOLY TRINITY
Onion, garlic, tomato

THE CHICKEN OR THE HEN?
Asare likes a tough bird

FATHER ASARE DANKWAH SATISFIES THE HUNGRY HEART: "My mother had four boys and then a girl and then me. Back home, cooking is supposed to be like women's job, but because my mother never had girls, she started teaching all the boys how to be self-sufficient and how to cook. My mother sold secondhand clothing in a store, so we had to prepare dinner at home. I thought it was great because I took pride in it. Not many of my friends know how to cook, and my home became like the company area. It has been a blessing in a way, because when I was at St. Monica's for six years, the parish could not afford to have a cook so I said, 'I don't need no cook. I can do my own cooking.'

"I came here from Ghana in 1987. That's a long time. I've been in New Orleans since all this time. Here I learned some creative ways, a combination of what I used to do back home and what people do here, like the seasonings, I see what combinations will give me a good taste. I've learned how to cook shrimp Creole and shrimp scampi, which I didn't do back home. I make my own sauce and just buy the shrimp. I don't follow a recipe. I use my own imagination. That's how we cook back home. Some people have to go by the book, but I don't do that.

After mass, Father Asare spends most of this Sunday afternoon making peanut butter soup and rice balls.

"Back home, people eat seafood like in New Orleans because seafood is cheaper. Beef and chicken is expensive. It is only the rich who can eat beef in Ghana, only the rich. Other people eat chicken on occasion, like Sundays, but seafood is the most common for ordinary people. You make your soup, either peanut butter soup from original peanuts or light soup with eggplant and cayenne pepper, onion, and tomatoes, and add whatever seafood you want to put in. Then you pour it on your bowl of fufu and you enjoy it.

"The most common food where I grew up is fufu. It's a mixture of cassava and plantain. You cook it and you pound it to make it soft. Here in the U.S. they've been able to make it the powder form and all you have to do is put the water on the fire, bring it to a boil, put the starch in, and mash it up like mashed potatoes.

"In Ghana, everything is prepared fresh. What is not eaten up at dinner is consumed at breakfast or lunch. Dinner is always prepared fresh. You see, not every household has a refrigerator. So you cook what you can consume that evening. When I came here I had a tough time getting used to leftovers.

"The food here in New Orleans is very similar to the food we eat in Ghana. People like spicy food here, and most people like spicy food in Ghana. Jambalaya, we have similar food that we call jollof rice. It's the same. Like gumbo, we have the same soup in Ghana. We don't call it gumbo, but we make soup just like gumbo and we eat it with rice, like here. Okra soup, people often have okra soup in Ghana.

"When I first came here, I was eating grits with milk and sugar like in Ghana. Not many people can afford to buy butter and eggs and all that. Milk is not that expensive. Sugar is cheap. But I stopped doing that. Now I eat grits as a New Orleanian. With butter, but I don't put no hot sauce.

"When I go home I try to bring some things. Once a year, I take my vacation and I get together with my friends and say, 'Okay, let me do something.' I will bake them some chicken with seasonings from here and they will really enjoy it. Even when I go visit some friends in New York or somewhere. 'Let's do something New Orleans.'

"When I grew up, the whole family would sit at a round table with one big bowl. You'll be eating from the same bowl, that's what I grew up with. Everybody eating together, it's just like the Eucharist. We all eat together. Sometimes, when you are mad at somebody, you feel very bad to go eat with that per-son. You have to reconcile before you go eat. If you are four people eating, the oldest person will divide the meat according to four and let each person take one. So if I'm the oldest, I would divide, but since I'm the oldest, I would take the last one, so there wouldn't be any cheating. It's not just the sharing of the meal. It begins a lesson, that you have to be fair in dealing with each other, you know, and also how to think of the other person, the younger one among you, because he is like the vulnerable one. And the oldest one is like the leader. Jesus said that the leader among you should be the one who serves, so it is a lesson not to be self-centered, to think of the other person."

—*As told by Asare Dankwah*

The Most African City in the U.S.

New Orleans culture and cuisine have strong connections to Africa because most of the slaves who came to Louisiana through the French slave trade shared the same languages and traditions and were able to hold on to some of them here. Two-thirds of the slaves came from the area between the Senegal and Sierra Leone rivers, sometimes called Greater Senegambia. New Orleans's West African food heritage is perhaps most visible in okra gumbo. Okra is literally called *gombo* in French and several African languages, such as *kingombo* in Kimbundu, a Bantu language spoken in Angola. The little green vegetable came to the New World from Africa, along with watermelon and black-eyed peas. Southern cooking also owes much to African cooking techniques, such as deep-frying. The Creole ladies who used to wander around the French Quarter selling calas, rice fritters, are long gone, but you can still buy similar fried buns, made from rice, millet, or corn, in West African marketplaces today.

Peanut Butter Soup
with Hen and Habañero

"Most of the time when I want to cook chicken, I want hen. Because chicken, before you've finished it, it falls apart." If you want to make this recipe with chicken, you should add the chicken at the end, about 45 minutes before serving. And remember, habañero pepper is very spicy.

6-pound hen, whole with skin and bones
1 lemon, cut in half
2 teaspoons Season-All
2 teaspoons Mrs. Dash Garlic & Herb
1 teaspoon poultry seasoning
1 head garlic, minced
3-inch piece fresh ginger, peeled and minced
1 yellow onion, diced
1 fresh habañero pepper
2 very large tomatoes
1 cup peanut butter (Asare prefers creamy)

Cut the hen into smaller pieces, removing excess fat and skin. Clean hen in water with lemon, rinse, and discard lemon. Put hen in a big pot with 1 inch water and dry seasonings. Cover and cook over medium fire about 20 minutes. Add onion, garlic, and ginger. Stir. Add the whole habañero and the two whole tomatoes and let them steam for 20 minutes, covering the dish. Then remove the stem from the habañero and puree with tomatoes in a blender. Return to pot. Liquify peanut butter in blender with 2 cups of water. Pour this into a separate pot, adding 2 more cups of water. Bring to a boil and simmer uncovered for about 20 minutes until thickened, then add to soup. Simmer soup for at least 1 hour. Serve with fufu or rice balls.

Fufu

Asare usually buys fufu flour and adds hot water according to the directions on the box. Fufu can also be made from scratch with fresh plantains and either cassava or yam (and strong arms!). Yam comes in all colors and sizes but should not be confused with sweet potato, which isn't a true yam. African yams are often hard to find in the U.S. but you can experiment with other yams. The consistency of fufu should be more like chewy dumplings than mashed potatoes. To make it from scratch, take 5 green plantains and 2½ cups cassava (also called manioc or yuca) or yam. Peel, cut into chunks, and cover with water in a large pot. Bring to a boil and simmer for 20–30 minutes until tender. Drain. Put the pot back on the stove over low heat and pound and stir the mixture with a sturdy wooden spoon or large wooden pestle for 15–20 minutes, adding a little water as you work so the mixture doesn't stick to the pot. When fufu is smooth and feels a bit like chewing gum, roughly shape into balls (the size of tennis balls) by wetting a round bowl with high edges and vigorously rolling each ball of fufu in it for a few seconds. Serve. Asare's parishioner Reine Pema Sanga from Benin figured out that you can make fufu with a KitchenAid mixer as well, using the flat beater. Work fufu at medium speed for 10–15 minutes, adding hot or cold water the same way. For softer consistency, add more water.

Rice Balls

Prepare white rice according to your regular recipe, but add extra water and overcook it slightly. Mash the rice in a large pot over low heat with a sturdy wooden spoon or large wooden pestle for 10 minutes, adding a little water as you work so the rice doesn't stick to the pot. Roughly shape into balls (the size of tennis balls) by dropping big dollops into a wet, round bowl with high edges, quickly and vigorously rolling each rice ball for a few seconds to perfect its shape. Serve.

New Orleans Slave Cooks

In the existing records of slaves in the Louisiana Slave Database, there are 665 entries about slave cooks in Orleans Parish between 1726 and 1820. Seventy percent of them were women. They were primarily Louisiana or New Orleans Creole (103)—that is, born here—but many of them were born in Congo (29) or St. Domingue/Haiti (26). If grouped together, all slave cooks born in Africa account for 102, rivaling the Creoles. During the Spanish period, there was a clear preference among slaveholders for Creole cooks (62 percent), while the majority of slave cooks during the early American period were born either in Africa or the Caribbean. Female cooks of certain ethnicities were especially popular, such as Wolof (Senegal and Gambia), Aja/Fon/Arada (roughly Benin), Mina (Togo), Igbo (Nigeria and Cameroon), and Congo. Exact birthplace, however, is given for less than 40 percent. There are also 98 records of slaves who were primarily bakers, confectioners, or chocolate makers in New Orleans, whereof only 9 were women. Slaves who could cook, bake, and make sweets were listed primarily as cooks, while slaves listed as bakers and confectioners generally did not cook. Eight slaves were listed as expert bakers, namely Mars, LaFleur, Segon, Rosette, Figaro, Pierre, Coffee, and Estevan.

Estevan was twenty-eight years old when he was sold in 1790, and, besides being an expert baker, he was also listed as a skilled carpenter, roofer, and mason. Among the expert cooks, there was Adele from St. Domingue, "of excellent character," who was sold in 1818 at age twenty-five for $2,425. She was the most expensive of all the cooks in her age group sold that year, almost twice as expensive as the second-most-expensive female cook, and three times as expensive as the average female slave. She must have been some *cuisinière*! There was also Felix from Mozambique, described as a good middle-class cook ("*fesant* [sic] *assez bien la cuisine bourgeoise*") who had spent some time in St. Domingue and was sold in New Orleans at age thirty in 1811. Among the average cooks, Victoria, most likely a Louisiana Creole, purchased her own freedom for five hundred pesos at age twenty in 1794. Many slave women made money by selling foods and sweets in the streets of the French Quarter. Most of this money went to their masters, but the vendors were able to save some, especially if they worked on Sundays, the slaves' day off in colonial Louisiana. Among the 39 slaves listed primarily as street vendors, only two were men.

Manila in the Chocolate City

"I cook Filipino food and I told my children, 'Y'all are picky? Y'all going to starve.'"

MINDA BAKER'S FAMILY LOVES HER FILIPINO FARE: "You know, in my country we eat with our hands. I still do it here, but I don't want to show nobody because they say 'savage.' They say, 'You don't bite it?' I say, 'Why? Why you going to bite it? Put your food in your mouth and chew it!' So we only do it in the house. We only eat with a fork when there's a fiesta, a wedding, or a birthday. Christmas we use fork. After that, we put our fork and spoon away until the next occasion comes. In my country, we use fork and spoon at special occasions only. When you have visitors coming, they use your special fork. Hospitable, that's what we call ourselves.

"My husband is from New Orleans. My husband was in the air force in the Philippines. I worked for him as a housekeeper. I was scared of him, because he's a big, black guy, okay? But then, New Year's Day I got a kiss. I wasn't breathing, because I didn't know how to kiss. He told me, 'Breathe, or you're going to die.'

"My mother-in-law, we used to live next to each other, like neighbors. I tell you about my mother-in-law, she's the best. When I first came here

Luzviminda Alfaro Baker

BORN
1964 in San Fernando, Pampanga, the Philippines

NEIGHBORHOOD
Broadmoor

OCCUPATION
Casino dealer

HOLY TRINITY
Soy sauce, vinegar, tomato

AMERICAN FOOD?
Snickers!

in 1990, my mother-in-law cooked for us for five months. She cooked red beans and rice, she baked chicken, she cooked gumbo; she cooked jambalaya and vegetable soup and spaghetti with crawfish. I was blessed with the best mother-in-law.

"Mostly I cook Filipino food. I cook adobo. Adobo is the most popular food Americans know in my country, the GI knows adobo. You can cook it with pork or chicken. You put vinegar and soy sauce and you put garlic, onion, potatoes, carrots, and bell pepper. You put it together in one pot and let it boil, let it boil, let it boil. My husband loves it. My mother-

When Minda makes her egg rolls and Filipino fish dishes, her sons, Luther, Jr., and Raymond, come into the kitchen every few minutes to look for samples.

in-law asked me how to cook adobo, so now she cooks adobo sometimes. Once you finish boiling, it's cooked. That's how easy it is.

"I make kare-kare, the oxtail. I boil the oxtail. I boil it and boil it and boil it and boil until it's tender. I put snap beans, I put eggplants, I put bok choi, and I put onion. I boil it and boil it and boil it and boil. At the end, when it's cooked, I put peanut butter to thicken the juice. I put peanut butter to thicken it. And then you pour it on your rice. When I cook that, my children eat and eat and eat.

"We eat a lot of fish so we cook a lot of fish. Meat is very, very expensive in the Philippines. They only sell beef on Wednesday and Saturday. That's it. If you want beef you have to wait on those days. Here, you go to Wal-Mart or Winn-Dixie. Beef all over!

We eat everything with rice. In my country we eat rice in the morning, at noon, and at night. Everything I'm telling you has rice on the side. That's why, when I came here, I felt at home because a lot of people eat rice. I always have rice at home because my children are looking for rice too. I taught them how to eat rice.

"I just cooked nilaga. Nilaga means boil. It's our everyday food in my country that I try to bring here. It's chicken or neck bones. I like neck bones. I put potatoes and cabbage or bok choi and you boil it and boil it and boil it again. Then you put salt and eat over hot rice. We call it nilaga, boil. It's very, very simple.

"Egg rolls, I make Filipino egg rolls. Sometimes it takes me all night to wrap them, because I just cannot make no twenty-five or thirty. I only make it once in a while, once in a blue moon. They are really, really good. If I make egg rolls I have to make more than a hundred, because if my neighbor find out that I make egg roll and I did not give her, I'm going to hear from her. My mother-in-law find out that I make egg roll and I didn't offer her none, I'm going to hear from her. If my sister-in-law and my nephews find out that I make some but didn't give them none, I am going to hear from them, so I have to make sure that everybody gets some and everybody be happy. And when I start frying, here comes my children, back and forth to the kitchen,

five in each hand. I just laugh, because I don't tell them they cannot take that. I just let them have them, so I make enough so they can eat their heart out."

—*As told by Minda Baker*

Egg Rolls (Lumpia)

These Filipino egg rolls are small and call for round and very thin wrappers. "They're very, very delicate so don't feel bad when you tear one." Minda's mother-in-law likes minced garlic in hers. Minda's sons usually eat their egg rolls with ketchup.

Makes 150

150 (about 3 packages) spring roll wrappers, frozen
4½ pounds ground beef
4 bunches green onions, sliced very thin
8 carrots, peeled and cut into itty-bitty cubes
2 tablespoons Season-All
2 + 4 eggs
Vegetable oil for deep-frying

Defrost wrappers. Mix ground beef with green onions, carrots, and Season-All, using hands. Beat 2 eggs separately and add to beef mixture. Mix thoroughly. Crack 4 eggs into a separate bowl—this will be used as "glue" to close egg rolls. Take out and separate only a few wrappers at a time, being careful not to let them dry out. Place a 2½-inch log of beef filling (about 2 tablespoons) horizontally across the bottom of each sheet. Roll twice, then fold in sides (like a burrito) and continue to roll, finally brushing egg "glue" onto the last 2 inches of the sheet to close egg roll. When about 10 egg rolls are ready, fry them and taste them to check if you need more seasonings.

Fish with Egg and Tomato (Sarciado)

This is one of Minda's sons' favorite dishes. Frying the fish involves some risk, so watch out for splashing. "Put the fish in and run!"

Serves 4 hungry sons or 8 adults

2 fresh tilapia, cleaned and scaled and cut crosswise into
    1½-inch-thick pieces (with skin and bones)
1 teaspoon salt
¼ cup vegetable oil
1 onion, thinly sliced
4 cloves garlic, mashed
10 tomatoes, sliced
½ tablespoon salt
3 cups water
4 eggs

Sprinkle salt over fish, and fry on all four sides until browned in oil in a skillet. Watch so that fish doesn't blacken or burn. Move fried fish to a platter. Fry onion and garlic in remaining oil until golden, stirring all the time. Add tomatoes and simmer until tomatoes disintegrate, 10–15 minutes. Add salt and water and simmer again. Add eggs, one at a time, stirring well. Add fish and simmer 5 more minutes. Serve over rice.

The Good Books

"I eat pretty healthy and I eat New Orleans food every day."

Kathleen Elise Fallon

BORN
1948 in New Orleans, Louisiana

NEIGHBORHOOD
Marigny

OCCUPATION
Retired realtor

HOLY TRINITY
Garlic, thyme, white wine

MALAISE?
Restaurant anxiety!

KAY FALLON GETS IN THE MOOD WITH COOKBOOKS AND WINE: "I'm not a gourmet cook. I don't do knockout standout food. It's just home-style cooking. I think of myself as a regular run-of-the-mill cooking person. If my food seems special it's because of the ingredients that I use and whatever I've garnered from the books that I've read.

"My mother was a businesswoman; she started her own business. Quite early, I guess I was about twelve, she would get tied up showing property and stuff and she would call up my sister and I and say, 'Start the shrimp Creole.' I remember the first couple of times, 'How are we going to cook that?!' She would say, 'Get *The Picayune Creole Cook Book* and read the recipe. If you can read, you can cook.' So that has always been my motto. If you can read, you can cook. I started following recipes and found that the Picayune book was a lot of fun. I read it like a novel. Little vignettes about the Creole lifestyle at the turn of the century. So that's pretty much how I learned how to cook.

"I was born in New Orleans at Touro hospital back in 1948 and lived on a plantation in Raceland, Louisiana, until I was about four. Then we moved back into town right behind my grandparents' house by Tulane University until I was seven, and then we moved to Covington. My mother was from

Kay leads the traditional blessing of the red beans and rice with her carnival krewe, the St. Anthony Ramblers, before each year's Mardi Gras parade. From left to right: Rose Sly, Alana Eager, Julia Garrison, Louis Dendinger, Richard Eager, Kay Fallon, Greg Garrison, Chris O'Brien, Cassady Cooper.

Covington and my father was from New Orleans. I grew up with cousins, uncles, and aunts on both sides of the lake. I spent a lot of time in New Orleans and a lot of time in Covington.

"When we lived on the plantation my mother had a two-acre vegetable garden that was tended by one of the helpers who lived on the plantation. We grew up on very fresh foods. We ate pretty much everything that was raised on the plantation. Chickens and different cows would be slaughtered, and most of the animals had names. I can remember the first time my mother ever served us hot dogs. My sister and I started crying hysterically because we wanted to know whom we were eating. We'd never had hot dogs before. 'Which dog are we eating, Mom?!' Big freak-out.

"The greatest thing my mother did for me is that she instilled the joy of cooking and the joy of reading cookbooks. Now I pick up an interesting cookbook and just sit down and read it from cover to cover. It's not that I actually follow recipes anymore, I get ideas of how recipes go and then I'll do things. I rarely pull out a recipe, unless it's something like a cake.

"My son was interested in cooking at an early age. I worked, and sometimes I would come home and put out left-overs and he didn't like that. So I said, 'If you think you can do better, you cook!' I had a bag of frozen vegetables for gumbo in the freezer, and he pulled that out and he pulled out some sausage. He made gumbo, at nine. Couldn't have been more than nine. He didn't make the roux, but he made a passable gumbo with okra in it. Overall I was very impressed. Now he loves to cook. He cooks differently than me, though. He cooks with the recipe book open on the counter. He's always trying new recipes and new styles of cooking, like Thai and Vietnamese. I've always used my mother's phrase with him, 'If you can read, you can cook.'

"When I cook I have to start with a glass of wine. It's hard for me to be standing over the stove if I haven't a glass of wine near to me. I remember hearing that a good cook has three glasses of wine. One when you sit down and decide what you're going to cook, one while you're cooking, and one with dinner. I always kind of adhered to that motto. A good glass of wine puts me in the mood. It also calms me down so I don't go scurrying around like a maniac and cut my finger off, which you can do if you get too stressed out and have to cook a big meal in a hurry. And I then want to have that in different dishes. I always put a little wine in the main course. Always have wine, whether it's gumbo or court bouillon or red beans. *Picayune Creole Cook Book* adds wine to everything, like a large coffee cup or a good claret wine glass, a demitasse cup. They didn't have measuring cups back then. A serving spoon of this or a soup spoon of that. They put wine in everything, and it enlivens the food and I also think helps preserve them. Really, I only drink two and a half glasses of wine when I cook."

—*As told by Kay Fallon*

Long Shelf Life

Kay's favorite cookbook, *The Picayune Creole Cook Book*, has been immensely popular since its first printing in 1900. Many of the recipes call for wine, which posed a problem after the passage of the Volstead Act in 1919 until the end of Prohibition in 1933. The 1936 edition came with the subtitle "Reprinted from the Fifth Edition, Containing Recipes Using Wines and Liquors Customary Before Prohibition," and the chapter temporarily named "Iced Fruit Drinks" was fully reinstated as "Domestic Wines, Cordials, Drinks."

Here are Kay's five favorite cookbooks and some of the recipes in them that she likes:

1. *The Original Picayune Creole Cook Book* (The Times-Picayune Publishing Company, New Orleans, LA, 1947)—oyster soup, turtle soup, gombo aux herbes, red beans and rice, grillades, cold daube a la Creole, bread pudding with lemon sauce, orange ice cream (for which Kay uses Louisiana navel oranges).

2. *Louisiana Cookery* by Mary Land (Claitor's Publishing Division, Baton Rouge, LA, 1972, copyright 1954 by the LSU Press)—oysters Bienville, coon vin ordinaire (which calls for "dago" red wine), pralines, squirrel stew. (Kay says, "It's like cooking rats, but squirrel has an interesting flavor.")

3. *Cane River Cuisine* (The Service League of Natchitoches, Inc., 1974)—marinated crab claws, shrimp dip, court bouillon, turkey bone gumbo, crawfish remoulade.

4. *Ten Talents* by Frank J. Hurd and Rosalie Hurd (The College Press, Tennessee, 1968)—carrot-rice loaf with cashew milk gravy, almond-lentil patties, walnut oat burgers, soy-millet patties, almond milk, best-barley soup, stuffed baked mushrooms.

5. *Recipes and Reminiscences of New Orleans Volume II: Our Cultural Heritage* (Ursuline Academy Parents' Club, 1981)—spinach oyster casserole, eggplant fritters, corn and crab soup, mint julep, chicken sauce piquante.

Stuffed Artichoke

Kay makes several versions of this recipe, replacing the olives with either 4 ounces canned tiny shrimp (drained) or half a box of fresh mushrooms, from which she removes the stems, slicing and sautéing the heads in olive oil before she adds them to the rest of the ingredients.

Makes 1

1 nice artichoke, preboiled in plenty of salted water with 1 crushed garlic clove for 10–15 minutes (cut the top and stem off first)
4 tablespoons olive oil
1 cup chopped green onion
4 cloves garlic, chopped
½ cup chopped parsley
⅓ cup sliced black olives
½ cup Italian breadcrumbs
1 tablespoon anchovy paste
Several shakes Tony Chachere's Creole Seasoning
¼ cup white wine
1 fistful of fresh basil, coarsely chopped
1 dash of oregano, dried or fresh and finely chopped
¼ cup grated Romano cheese
1 tablespoon olive oil
2 tablespoons grated Parmesan cheese

Heat oil in a cast-iron frying pan. Add green onion and garlic and cook until soft. Add parsley, olives, breadcrumbs, anchovy paste, and Tony's, mixing well. Add wine. When breadcrumbs have soaked up wine, turn heat off. Add basil, oregano, and Romano cheese, mixing well. Place artichoke stem side down on a large piece of aluminum foil. Pull out center leaves and scrape out artichoke hair with a spoon, discarding these. Stuff artichoke center first, then outer, bottom leaves, working your way up and around. When all the leaves are stuffed, press remaining stuffing into the top of the artichoke. Drizzle oil on top and finish with Parmesan cheese. Wrap the foil tightly around the artichoke and place in 1 inch boiling water in a large pot. Cover and steam for 20–40 minutes until you can pull leaves out easily.

Daube Glacé

Kay got this recipe from her mother, who used to make it for Christmas and New Year's Eve. If you can't get pigs' feet, several envelopes of unflavored gelatin mixed into 2 quarts of heated beef broth will work, but is not as good as pigs' feet. Daube glacé is basically a fancy version of hogshead cheese.

Serves 30

4 pounds veal or beef roast
3 pounds lean pork roast
4 cloves garlic, sliced
Creole seasoning (cayenne, black pepper, salt, garlic powder, thyme)
¼ cup oil
8 pigs' feet
4 quarts water
1 tablespoon balsamic vinegar
3 yellow onions, diced
4 ribs celery, diced
1 cayenne pepper, sliced
2 bell peppers, diced
2–4 tablespoons brandy or dry sherry
1 bunch green onions, chopped
1 bunch parsley, chopped (without stems)

Make slits in roasts, fill with sliced garlic, and season with Creole seasoning. Heat oil in a large cast-iron pot and brown meat on all sides. Cover and place in a 325 degree oven for about 2 hours. While roasts are cooking, add pigs' feet to water with vinegar and boil uncovered for 1 hour to make 6–8 cups

of gelatin. Discard feet. You can test the stiffness of the gelatin by pouring a small amount into a shallow dish and placing it in the refrigerator until cold. Sprinkle diced onion, celery, cayenne pepper, and bell pepper over roasts. Add brandy. Cover and cook about 30 minutes more. Add green onions and parsley, stir, and set aside to cool. Shred meat with hands, using a knife to cut longer strings, mixing well with pan juices. Place in two large molds or several small molds. Cover with gelatin mixture. Place molds in refrigerator overnight or longer until firm. To serve, dip bottom of mold into warm water briefly, and then run a thin knife around rim of mold. Turn upside down on serving plates and enjoy with thinly sliced baguette, red wine or chilled dry champagne.

Setting the Story

"You've got one cup for the white man. The Indian drinks out of the bottle."

PETER COUSIN MAKES PEACE WITH THE PAST: "My mother had seven sons and two daughters, and she made all of us work in the kitchen and learn how to cook. She said, 'When you leave here you gonna know how to scrub, how to wash, how to cook, how to do everything you're supposed to do in the kitchen. That's my law.' Yes, ma'am.

"My people started over in France, the Cousins. But there is also Choctaw on my father's side. My mother was French and she didn't like the Indians. She didn't want us to socialize with them, but we did it anyhow. She wanted us to *parlez-vous français*, like her.

"The Indian part, we kind of kept it hid, because way back then it wasn't kosher to be Indian. But when I started researching my heritage, I found out that my great paternal grandfather had two Choctaw wives.

"My paternal grandmother's father was a white man, and I think her mama was a black woman, or slave. She bought her mama's freedom, or the old man gave her her mama, she was from Pearl River. She left and came down here. She had that old black lady with her. Took good care of her too.

"Way back before they had baby food, those black ladies used to take the food and put it in their mouths and chew it up and then put it in the baby's

Peter McNeil White Fox Cousin, Sr.

BORN
1927 in Lacombe, Louisiana

LIVES IN
Lacombe

OCCUPATION
Retired contractor

HOLY TRINITY
Garlic, parsley, paprika

SECRET SKILLS?
Quilts and filé

Peter gathers sassafras leaves in the summer. He makes filé for the ladies in Lacombe who are wary of store-bought counterfeits that are cut with bay leaf.

mouth, let the baby eat it. Did it for the whites, you know, they raised them children, the white women didn't raise them children on the plantation. That was a known fact. And my mama said, 'Be damn, that old black lady ain't chewing no food and putting in my children's mouths!' She just didn't like that process.

"Creole is a culture. We all hung together, a whole group of people that was kind of mixed-blooded people. And of course my father was accepted amongst everybody because his daddy looked just like a white man. My daddy said, 'First thing you gotta do, you gotta learn how to fight, because there's going to be some people out there messing with you.' He learned all boys

how to fight and how to shoot. We hunted every year. Deer and turkey and quail and ducks, all kind of stuff like that. My father told us, 'You need to be a good shot,' because when you're going a-huntin' that's your dinner you're looking at.

"The Indian had to eat what he could find. You hunt something, kill something, or grow something. And that was it. I used to have a nice garden. I raised tomatoes, cucumbers, greens, spinach, mustard, collard greens, turnips, beets, cauliflower, and broccoli. And cabbage, I'd grow some nice cabbage.

"I don't cook with a recipe. I cook with talent. I just know how I want it to taste. I got it in my head some kind of way. The best way to cook is to have not too much heat. Most people put too much heat under their food, and they burn it. I always cook on a slow fire. We all learned how to cook on a wood stove. Later on we got them gas stoves, and we had to learn to cook all over again. Gas and wood are altogether different. A wood stove stays the same temperature as long as you keep wood in it.

"There are all kinds of old tricks in cooking. You take the venison and put some vinegar on it, salt, and you let it stay in some water overnight, take the wild taste out of it. The trick about frying fish is you put some lemon juice on your fish, that's the Creole style, put your salt and pepper and everything. Then you put your fish-fry on there and you cover it. Let it stay about forty, fifty minutes so the moisture will come out of that fish and wet the fish-fry and the fish-fry will stick to the fish. But if you put your fish-fry on there and then put it in the hot grease right away it all come off. And the fish-fry will burn in the grease and give your fish a bad taste. That's another trick you gotta know.

"You're talking about two nations. There are the European settlers and the Choctaws. Every now and then they would have a dispute. Then they would have to have a meeting with the chief and a peace setting with Indian corn bread, roast venison, venison sausage, fried Indian bread, roast sweet potatoes, or succotash. They'd have a plate and a fork and a cup for the settler, and the Indian's plate was made out of palmetto leaves. And after everything was settled, everybody would take a drink of homemade Indian wine."

—As told by Peter Cousin

The Pot Thickens

Many people know that the name "gumbo" comes from an African word for okra, since slaves introduced the small, green vegetable to local cuisine. But some people believe there is more to the name of New Orleans's favorite soup. While okra was used as a thickener in gumbo half the time, filé was an equally good alternative. Filé (from French *fil*, thread, referring to how filé can make soups stringy) was ground from sun-dried sassafras leaves in the fall and brought to New Orleans marketplaces by Choctaw Indians who lived on the other side of Lake Pontchartrain. According to David I. Bushnell, Jr., who wrote about the Choctaw of Bayou Lacombe one hundred years ago, the Choctaw name for ground sassafras is *kombo' ashish*, leading people to believe that the name "gumbo" might have come from Native American filé. But this is probably not true. The Choctaw name for sassafras is *kafi'*. Native Americans mainly used sassafras for tea and medicine, and in Koasati, a cousin language, *hassi* means plant or weed. Bushnell's *ashish* probably means dried leaves or herbs to be infused in hot water, while *kombo'* most likely refers to okra or gumbo, since the Chickasaw word for okra is *kombo'*. *Kombo' ashish* could therefore mean "dried herbs used for gumbo" or "dried leaves that act like okra." Filé gumbo has been prepared in New Orleans at least since 1764 when two West African female street vendors mentioned the dish in a testimony.

Muscadine Wine

"White muscadine grapes. You take 'em and you bust 'em, put a little water on 'em and a little bit of sugar and you let them ferment for six days in a crock, it got to be a clay crock. Then you add your water, however percentage you want your wine to be at, and I think it's two and a half pounds of sugar per gallon of liquid. You take it and you put it in jugs, you put a cork in the jug and you put a tube down in through the cork, and you put paraffin around it so no air can't get in. And you take the tube and you run it into a cup of water and as that stuff ferments it makes bubbles in that cup and no air can get back in to spoil your wine. And when you see it stop bubbling, you pull the tube out and you cap it. You wrap it up in a piece of black cloth and put it somewhere in the closet where there is no light and let it stay in there about three to four months. If it's good, say it's good. If it's bad, say it's bad. But it's a *bon petit vin*."

Succotash

This recipe includes both green onions and shallots, which might confuse some Louisianans who call green onions (also known as scallions) shallots. This confusion probably arose when the French settlers in and around New Orleans found green onions to be a good replacement for shallots. Many Louisiana versions of French sauces (bordelaise, marchand de vin, ravigote) substitute garlic and green onions for shallots. Peter cooks succotash without salt, minding his pressure, but likes to eat it with hot sauce. He uses mushroom or chicken broth for liquid most of the time, "but if you want it to taste like the Indian thing, you add water."

Serves 4

2 tablespoons vegetable oil
2 tablespoons flour
1 yellow onion, diced
3–4 shallots, chopped
2–3 green onions, chopped
1 tablespoon minced garlic
Chopped ham
1 cup water or broth
1 can yellow corn, drained
1 can baby lima beans, drained
1 tablespoon chopped parsley

Make a roux by heating the oil in a cast-iron pan, adding flour and cooking, stirring constantly, over low heat until the roux is any shade of brown. Add onion, shallots, green onions, and garlic and sauté for a few minutes. Add ham, liquid, corn, and beans and simmer over low heat for about 20 minutes. Add parsley. Serve warm as a side dish.

Papaya on the Bayou

"In America, I learned how to grow more Vietnamese stuff than in Vietnam."

CHIN THI NGUYEN STRUGGLES TO GROW HER NATIVE CROPS IN THE HARSH LOUISIANA WINTERS: "My name is Chin Thi Nguyen. I am sixty-seven years old. I came to the U.S. in 1975, after the fall of Saigon. My little city, Vung Tau, had lots of water and boats. It was a fishing community.

"We use many herbs in our cooking. Mint leaves, the different types of mint leaves. The basil leaf, the mint, the purple basil, and cilantro. Vietnamese watercress, that's what we eat the most. I grow watercress and bean sprouts, green leaf lettuce, and mustard greens.

"And I grow papaya. The papaya tree, every year, it is either small or it dies. But I really like papaya, because we eat it in salad. That's the one thing I miss. Papaya tree. It's too cold here in the winter. It has to be perfect weather all year. We had papaya all year round in Vietnam. But here, as soon as it gets cold, it dies. We trim it, but it takes forever to grow back again. You have to wait so long, hoping that the next year, fruit will come out. But it gets cold, and you have no fruit. It takes a while to get fruit. About four years ago, we had a hot winter and we had big papaya. It was beautiful. But that was it. That's the last time we saw it. I get mad.

Chin Thi Nguyen

BORN
1937 in Vung Tau, Vietnam

LIVES IN
Marrero

OCCUPATION
Homemaker

HOLY TRINITY
Fish sauce, soy sauce, black pepper

SECRET LOVE?
Bottled spring water!

"Persimmon is one of the main fruits in Vietnam. They can grow here. We have a great big persimmon tree. It covers the whole house. I have a special technique so it doesn't be bitter. When the fruit is about to be ripe, you put the persimmon in a brown paper bag and throw apples in there and the apples soak up the bitterness. And if you split the apple in half it has turned black. You leave the fruit in the bag for about three days. The cheapest apples you can get.

"I lost my parents when I was one, so I learned about gardening from other people. In Vietnam, the family, you only have one certain task. They only let me grow one thing. Papaya.

Chin is the last one in her family in America who gardens. None of her seven children or grandchildren wants to learn. In the foreground, daughter-in-law Sophie Tran.

"My cooking did not change a lot when we came to America. I eat the same thing, but we have more electricity here. I have kept the same techniques, because all the ingredients are here. It has gotten much easier. In 1975, we couldn't even get the fish sauce, so it was really hard. That's why it was so important for us to start gardening here. That's why we started farming ourselves. We had chickens to do the eggs, things like that. Later on, I want to say in 1978, this one Vietnamese man opened the first grocery store and carried all the little Vietnamese products. Vietnamese people were flocking just to go there. In the beginning we were forced to cook the American way. They gave us commodities from the government. They gave us Spam and corned beef hash and powdered milk and government cheese. Uncle Ben's rice, we are not used to that. The rice is like falling apart. We had to eat American most of the time, but we used a lot of soy sauce and just mixed that in. But it didn't taste the same.

"There was always access to sugar in Vietnam, through the sugarcane. We made our own rice and our sugar. That's why there was a major population coming down to Louisiana. We came through the United Catholic Charities, we all were. They told us that Louisiana would be the best place if you were used to the humidity, the weather, the fishing, and all that. Some families went up north. My friend and her family, they just picked Ohio and oh, my goodness, what regret.

"The strangest thing I ever ate in America is chicken that are grown in a farm and frozen. We kill our own chicken and eat it fresh, so it's a different taste. Frozen chicken, when you cook it, is mushy. Fresh chicken still has its texture; it's a wilder taste.

"Turnips and sweet potatoes are Vietnamese vegetables. That's one of the things we eat a lot. In Vietnam, in 1975, the Communist government took over Vietnam. And here you have the Communists saying, you can't have this land, you work for me and I'm selling the rice and make the money off of it. So all my family and any Vietnamese family that was left in 1975, they decided to rebel by not making rice at all. They sacrificed. For about ten years, they did not eat rice. They only ate sweet potato. Finally, the people won. They got their land back. Anyone over here, Vietnamese people love potatoes. But anyone who had to go through that, during the war, they can't stand potatoes."

—As told by Chin Thi Nguyen,
translated by her daughter-in-law Sophie Tran

Welcome to Versailles

New Orleans East is home to the densest Vietnamese population in the world outside Vietnam. The Vietnamese community has made its most impressive post-Katrina recovery in the area called Versailles and Village de l'Est. More than 80 percent of the residents have returned, and the famous front and backyard gardens—killed by salt water and prolonged flooding after Katrina—are sprouting up, together with plans for a large community garden next to Mary Queen of Vietnam Church. Some of the most popular herbs and vegetables grown in these gardens are lemongrass; spearmint; Thai basil; Chinese chives, celery, and cabbage; kohlrabi; red hot peppers; mustard and collard greens; green onions; gourds; yellow onions; taro; water spinach; and Malabar spinach.

Chicken Noodle Soup (Pho Ga)

This is a beautiful, simple soup. Don't overload your bowl with noodles or meat; bring them in for the chorus, but let the broth sing the verse. If you can find fresh rice noodles at a local Asian supermarket, use them! This recipe calls for dried noodles since they're much easier to find. You will probably not use more than half the chicken meat when you serve this soup, so save the rest for stir-fry or chicken salad.

Serves 5

For the broth:
1 whole chicken, cut in half
1 yellow onion, cut in half
3–4 star anise
4-inch piece fresh ginger root, unpeeled
Cheesecloth
Salt and sugar to taste (about 2 teaspoons salt and 2 tablespoons sugar)

For serving:
14 ounces rice stick noodles (banh pho)
2 green onions, chopped
Yellow onion shavings
Cilantro, chopped
Basket of fresh bean sprouts, sliced hot peppers, Thai basil,
lime wedges

Remove excess fat from chicken and put in a large pot with more than enough water to cover (about 10 cups). Bring to a boil. Cut the ginger in half lengthwise and wrap it up in cheesecloth with onion and star anise. Add to pot. Simmer for about 1 hour. Discard cheesecloth bag. Remove chicken from broth and let cool. Tear off and cut meat into pieces. Season broth with salt and sugar. Soak noodles in lukewarm water for about 20 minutes, until pliable. When ready to serve, put enough noodles for one in a sieve and dip into hot boiling water for a few seconds, drain, and put into serving bowl. Top with chicken pieces, green onions, yellow onion, and cilantro. Finally, add about 2 cups broth. Serve immediately with a basket of greens as well as hoisin sauce, Sriracha hot chili sauce (also called "rooster sauce"), and fish sauce for those who like sweeter, spicier, or saltier tastes.

Fresh Spring Rolls (Goi Cuon)

This is a great appetizer to eat on hot and humid days. You can add other things you like to the rolls, such as fresh herbs (mint, Thai basil) or carrot shavings or fresh bean sprouts—although the latter can make them harder to roll. Serve with dipping sauce; recipe below.

Makes 16 rolls, serves about 8

16 sheets Vietnamese rice paper (banh trang, large size, about
25 centimeters in diameter)
1 pound cold, cooked pork in thin, small slices
1 small head red leaf or green leaf lettuce, finely shredded
16 ounces thin Vietnamese rice stick noodles
32 cooked, peeled large shrimp, cut in half lengthwise (along
"backbone")

Soak noodles in lukewarm water for about 20 minutes, until pliable. Boil noodles for a few seconds, drain and rinse with cold water, shake out water, and set aside. For assembly, fill a large, wide bowl with water and dip 1 sheet of rice paper, turning paper if necessary. You can also just rinse the rice paper under the faucet. Lay it on the counter and it will soften in seconds. Put 1 or 2 slices of pork at 6 o'clock, at least 1 inch from the edge, spreading the pork straight across horizontally between 4 o'clock and 8 o'clock. Add a handful of lettuce over the pork. Next, add a handful of noodles (noodles should be sticky, not wet). Next, place 4 shrimp halves cut side up at 12 o'clock, leaving at least 1 inch to the edge, spreading shrimp straight across horizontally between 10 o'clock and 2 o'clock, as wide as bottom fillings go. Start rolling: fold bottom flap up over pork, lettuce, and noodles, stretching rice paper and compacting fillings as much as possible. The rice paper will stick to itself. Next, fold in right side of rice paper over bottom fillings and shrimp, then left side. You should be looking at a vertical rectangle with a rounded top. Now, continue to roll from the bottom up. Done!

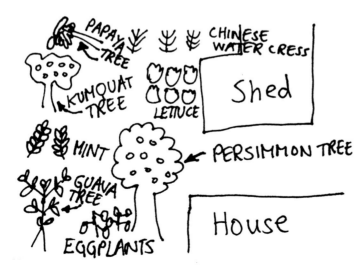

Drawing of the layout of her garden

Mung Bean Sweet Rice Dipping Sauce

This dipping sauce is easy to make without peanuts, if you don't like or are allergic to them.

1 cup split and dried mung beans
½ cup uncooked Thai sweet rice
1 tablespoon vegetable oil
2 cloves garlic, minced
½ cup hoisin sauce
1 tablespoon sugar
¼ cup water
Peanut butter (optional)
1 handful chopped or crushed dry roasted peanuts (optional)
Rooster sauce (Sriracha hot chili sauce)

Boil mung beans and sweet rice together in plenty of water until tender, drain. Put the bean and rice mixture in a blender with enough water to make a paste. You will only use ½ cup of this, so keep the rest in Ziploc bags in the freezer for later use. Next, fry garlic slowly in oil. Add hoisin and sugar and simmer for a few minutes. Mix this with the bean and rice blend and enough water (about ¼ cup) to reach dipping sauce consistency. If sauce gets too runny, you can thicken it with peanut butter. Serve the sauce warm or at room temperature with peanuts and rooster sauce on top. It is best to serve the sauce in several small dishes so that everyone can dip at the same time.

Pearls from Plaquemines

"We eat oysters two—three times a week,
but not as much as we should."

SNJEŽANA BJELIŠ MAKES HER FAMILY'S BED BETWEEN SALTY AND SWEET: "My husband came in, I think, it was 1981. I came in 1986. We married here, in Port Sulphur. We are from the same village in Croatia. We know each other from the childhood.

"My husband was not in the oyster industry before he came here. In Croatia, oysters are scarce. Where we come from is also by the riverbank so we have fields, oranges and fruits. That's where we worked. That's why we gravitated here to Louisiana. Water, water is to us natural; to travel by water, to work in water. He has a cousin here that came before him and one of his brothers, so it just came up as a simple solution. His father was a fisherman. He was fishing sardines in the Adriatic, same as my dad. There are maybe different opportunities in New Orleans, but you do what you think you know and will be good at and something that's familiar to you. It is him. It is us.

"Oysters grow where water is mixed, salty water and river water. My husband goes from one area to the next. If there are no oysters here, he goes where oysters are. That wasn't big deal when he was younger, but now it's not easy. My husband owns a fishing dock, it's right very close. He gets up at three or four, comes home at nine or ten, or ten thirty, then gets up at three.

Snježana Šeput-Bjeliš

BORN
1956 in Metković, Croatia

LIVES IN
Belle Chasse
(Empire pre-Katrina)

OCCUPATION
Sales associate at Williams-Sonoma

HOLY TRINITY
Olive oil, garlic, white wine

COOKING TIP?
Add butter

"I think oysters are good business. Oysters are like farming. You plant your oysters. You build a reef from empty shells. Eventually, you have your own spot where you can produce and sell in a good price in a good time.

"We never cooked oysters back in Croatia. Mussels we had in abundance and some other seashells, which grow in the sand. Croatian people come here to Louisiana to fish, and, of course, if they go back they bring their knowledge of harvesting oysters and apply that over there. They have some businesses over there now.

"Croatians are very food oriented. They don't stock food because they go in the morning shopping. Before work, they get

Snježana Bjeliš's husband, Mato, is very busy during oyster season from September to April and spends most of his time on his boat. In the summers, the family usually goes back to Croatia. Snježana negotiated three months' vacation time from her boss by baking him a double-chocolate torte.

up early. It's a way of life. People get up really early in Croatia, they go to the market, they get from the bakeries their French bread, everything smells, the whole town is full of aroma.

"Instead of butter on the bread with milk or with tea, we would spread lard and put a coarse sugar on top to make it sweet. If you like it salty, somebody would sprinkle sweet pepper, paprika. That's a meal right there. We ate butter in Croatia, but we're eating it more here because it's a good snack for children, instead of eating something junky. I prefer this for them. The good butter gives a great flavor. And I use so much olive oil, you wouldn't believe. One liter is still cheaper in Arabic store in New Orleans than in Croatia.

"As far as preserving and keeping on with my Croatian heritage I think it's because I'm stubborn. I want my children to eat soup on Sundays so we can have a family meal the way I think we should have it. It's okay if people don't do it that way, but that's the way I feel that we should have certain things. I don't buy sodas. They have water or lemonade or milk.

"I bake all kinds of sweets, mostly traditional. I'm going back to my roots. I like that old-fashioned Croatian stuff in cooking and baking. Also, I like to have beautiful old recipes. Older is sweeter. [Snježana pulls out a Croatian cookbook with recipes like punjena paprika, stuffed bell peppers; punjeni svinjski filet, stuffed pork chops; pečeni odojak, cochon de lait/roast suckling pig; palachinke, crêpes; and rolada sa marmaladom, jelly roll.]

"My children are boys, but they watch me do things. I even thought about translating my recipes in English for them and make a copy for each one so they will have it. Maybe their wives will like to cook, or maybe they will have time or desire to make them if they miss them or want them when they grow older.

"I stick to my mom's recipes, to the way I grew up. That's the way I raise my kids, that's the way I cook. That's the way it's familiar to me. I cook oysters my way. I don't know how other people cook it. I just cook it my own way, like I would cook it probably if I was home in Croatia.

"I hated oysters when I came here. I didn't want to even taste oysters. I didn't care. But later on when I tried them, I just fell in love with them. And I love them now; I simply love them.

"Our children are not very fond of seafood. But I know that it will come to them. They will love it. Because there is a smell . . . Oysters are present in our life, so it will come to them, they will come to love it. I know that through experience."

—*As told by Snježana Bjeliš*

1001 Dalmatians

Dalmatian fishermen and sailors began coming to New Orleans by the hundreds in the 1830s, leaving their homes along the Adriatic coast of present-day Croatia. Most of them came on vessels carrying goods from Europe to the United States and decided to jump ship once they reached port in New Orleans. Those who could not find jobs along the riverfront learned about oysters from fellow fishermen. Oyster farming came naturally to those from the Pelješac peninsula in Dalmatia where the best Adriatic oysters had been cultivated for centuries. To this day, Croatian oyster farmers in Louisiana transfer small seed oysters from public, natural reefs to private, protected bedding grounds, where the oysters get plenty to eat and grow fat and juicy.

Barbecued Oysters

This dish belongs somewhere between risotto and jambalaya, Croatia and New Orleans. Snježana usually serves this as an appetizer or a side dish.

Serves 4

1 pint oysters, shucked, in their own juice
5 tablespoons (or more) olive oil
2–3 cloves garlic, minced
Fresh parsley, chopped with stems
Fresh dill, chopped
½ cup uncooked basmati rice

Heat oven to 400 degrees. Place oysters, reserving juice, into a pan and bake them for a few minutes until they release some of their water. Take the pan out and turn oysters around in the liquid a few times. Pour oyster liquid and reserved juice through a sieve to get rid of any small pieces of shell that might be in there. Add olive oil, garlic, parsley, and fresh dill to oysters. Stir. Add rice and oyster juice/liquid. Stir. Put the pan back in the oven and bake for 10–15 minutes. Stir every few minutes. Serve plain or with grated Parmesan cheese.

Steamed Mussels

This dish is very quick and easy to prepare and tastes as good as most steamed mussels served in restaurants.

Serves 2

2 pounds fresh, live mussels
Salt for purging
¾ cup olive oil
1 yellow onion, chopped
3–4 cloves garlic, chopped
1 cup dry white wine
2 tablespoons chopped fresh oregano
4 tablespoons chopped fresh parsley
½ teaspoon salt
½ teaspoon freshly ground pepper
Juice of 1 lemon

Clean the closed mussels by washing and rubbing them with a stiff brush. Place mussels in salted water for about 30 minutes to discharge sand and dirt. Discard water. Pull beards off. Steam mussels open for 2–3 minutes over boiling water. In a large pot, heat oil, sautéing the onion and garlic until transparent. Add mussels, wine, oregano, parsley, salt, and pepper. Cover and cook for 5 minutes until practically all the mussels have opened, shaking the pan a few times. Sprinkle with lemon juice. Serve in large bowls.

London Squares (Londoneri)

"Nothing can go wrong," says Snježana about this Croatian recipe, since it does not call for baking powder, baking soda, or yeast. She whips her egg whites with a pinch of salt or a few drops of vinegar to ensure a stiff meringue.

Makes 16 squares

Biscuit:
1½ sticks butter
⅓ cup sugar
Zest of 1 lemon
3 egg yolks
1⅔ cups flour

Filling:
1 cup fairly stiff jam or marmalade (Snježana prefers apricot)

Meringue:
3 egg whites
1 cup sugar
5 ounces almonds or pecans, sliced or chopped

Preheat oven to 350 degrees. Line a medium square or rectangular baking pan with parchment paper, folding at corners. Mix butter, sugar, and lemon zest until creamy. Add egg yolks and flour and mix until you have an even dough, but do not overmix. With floured fingers, spread dough evenly in pan. Bake for 20–25 minutes until half-baked. When 5 minutes remain, prepare meringue. Whip egg whites until stiff. Add sugar and continue to whip until meringue forms peaks. Fold in most of the nuts. Spread jam or marmalade over biscuit. Spread meringue on top. Garnish with remaining nuts. Put the pan back in the oven until meringue top is dry and golden. This could take anywhere from 20 to 40 minutes, depending on your oven and the stiffness of the meringue. Cool completely. Remove from pan. Cut into squares.

Common Scents

"I'm very hybrid. Everything I make is a mix of cultures."

Alina Sierra Sedlander

BORN
1951 in Remedios, Cuba

LIVES IN
Metairie

OCCUPATION
Social worker

HOLY TRINITY
Cumin, garlic, lime

KITCHEN MATH?
New Orleans = beans + rice = Cuba

ALINA SEDLANDER SENSES SIMILARITIES BETWEEN NEW ORLEANS CUISINE AND THAT OF HER NATIVE CUBA: "I was born in Cuba, I lived there until I was ten. My father was a doctor. He had to start all over again, do all his training again here. I came to New Orleans to go to graduate school at Tulane. That was in 1974. But I love New Orleans. The French Quarter reminds me of the town I grew up in in Cuba, one of the five first colonial towns established after Columbus came. Our houses are just like the French Quarter. And the food here, it was so close to my heart, so different from any other city in the United States.

"Of course, Cuba's an island so there was seafood everywhere. We have shrimp Creole and jambalaya, something very similar. Cubans make a lot of rice with different things, sausage or shrimp. There's a lot of similarities. The beans. In New Orleans you have the white beans and the red beans. Ours, of course, is black beans. But we also like white beans and red beans, garbanzos, and all of those. Cubans don't have hot pepper, cayenne, in their red beans. Not in the red beans, no cayenne. The Cuban red beans have vegetables. Potatoes and calabasa, it's like pumpkin, and other vegetables and chorizo

Alina looks through cook-
books with her daughter,
Alexandra. She keeps her
mother's Cuban cookbook on
the highest shelf in the house,
in case of flooding.

sausage and tossino, the fat pork; garlic, onions, and green peppers. In New Orleans they use a lot of celery, we really don't use
a lot of celery. I use celery in my red beans because it's the New
Orleans way to do it, but I'm not crazy about celery. Cumin is
not used enough in most places. I just love it. We use it a lot.
Not in huge amounts, it's just like a speck, but you can taste it.

"I brought my mother's cookbook. We came from Cuba in
1960 and this is like *the* Cuban cookbook that everybody has.
It is like the Bible. My mother didn't know how to cook when
we came from Cuba. She had never cooked in her life, because
she had a cook in Cuba. All of a sudden, we came without any
money, so she had to learn how to cook. So what she did was,
she had somebody send her this cookbook and she turned out
to be a really good cook, although she hated and hates cooking.
She just passed her book down to me. My father used to say he
liked to watch me cook because I seemed to enjoy every part

of it. The smells, the feels. I'm a big hand washer, but I use my
hands a lot. I like to use my hands.

"My husband loves Cuban food. He took to it like crazy.
He helps me. I had polio as a child, so my mobility is limited.
He loves for me to cook, so he'll do anything to help me in the
kitchen.

"My mother, my sister, and my brothers live in Florida, and
we go to the beach every summer. I'm usually the one who ends
up cooking. And typically, what I make is a crawfish pasta dish
that I got from a friend of mine whose family is Cajun. My
family loves crawfish, everybody. They took to it like they'd lived
here all their lives. And usually I make New Orleans red beans.
When my father was alive, I would bring oyster and artichoke
soup. And shrimp, my family loves shrimp. I used to go with ten
pounds of frozen shrimp and make my mother's famous shrimp
enchilada, which is like shrimp Creole. Otherwise we would

have the pork that my mother made, with white rice, and usually with every meal my mother made fried plantains, which all of us are like crazy over. My mother's fried plantains are outstanding, and we all fight to get as many as possible. White rice and plantains with every meal.

"Sour orange or lime makes everything better. I use lime for meats, especially pork. To me, that makes all the difference. I use that a lot. Lime makes the meat more tender and gives it a wonderful, citrusy taste. My mother used to make juice ice cubes so she always would have it. I use lime for everything. Really. Literally. My husband knows to buy limes without asking me if we need any.

"So much of the food in New Orleans is African and Spanish. The same thing in Cuba, the Spanish and the African influence. I cook a mixture of Cuban and New Orleans food. That's really what I cook. So much is the same to me, except for the celery. We use the same basic stuff, you know. It is not only the architecture and everything, but the food, when I moved here, it felt so much like home.

"I love the Spanish food. In the recipes here in my mother's Cuban cookbook there is an Isleños soup, it says 'sopa isleña,' because a lot of families who came from the Canary Islands here, then they left and went to Cuba. A lot of my father's ancestors came from the Canary Islands. So there's a real connection. Some went directly to Cuba, but some stopped here and then they went to Cuba. Cuban food is very influenced by the Spanish. See, 'sopa isleña,' it's made with fish heads. It's got almonds, which is also very Spanish.

"This book came from Cuba, published in Cuba for Cubans by a Cuban woman who never left Cuba. And here's a recipe for Parisian green beans. With lime! And I've never heard of Polish cauliflower, but there it is. With lime! And here's dobos cake, it says Hungarian torte. This must be doberge, huh? Filled with chocolate and with caramel on top? I think there was a lot of back and forth between Cuba and New Orleans. Otherwise, you'd have to wonder how this recipe got into my mother's cookbook."

—*As told by Alina Sedlander*

Hog Love

Louisiana is often said to consume more pork than any other state in the union. Bacon fat is used as a seasoning and remains a kitchen fixture. Because we continue to use every part of a pig, including the head for hogshead cheese and the fatty skin for cracklings, Louisianans prefer a smaller but fatter pig, especially for whole hog roasts (cochon de lait). Louisiana's love for the hog could possibly be explained by the fact that the early settlers, the French, Spanish, and Germans, all came from sausage-loving countries. New Orleans ranked as number four among the leading sausage retail cities in the United States in 2006, according to Information Resources Inc. This was one year after Katrina, when the city was still a wreck and there was limited access to grocery stores, kitchens, electricity, and refrigerators. Pigs are not native to the New World, but came here with Christopher Columbus, who in 1493 let loose a Spanish hog on Cuba.

Headless Cochon de Lait

Cochon de lait is supposed to be roasted suckling pig, but Alina could never stand the idea. Instead, she makes this delicious version with pork tenderloins. Its magnificent glaze calls for Malta, which is a soft drink that tastes like a mixture of prune juice and molasses, and is available in the international foods aisle of many large supermarkets.

Serves 8

2 pork tenderloins
5 cloves garlic, mashed
Juice of 2 limes
Juice of 1 lemon
½ cup orange juice
1 teaspoon sea salt
1 teaspoon oregano
2 pinches of cumin
½ teaspoon black pepper
⅓ cup olive oil

For the glaze:
1 (12-ounce) bottle Malta
½ cup light brown sugar

Start the day before, as the pork needs to marinate overnight. Put the whole tenderloins and the rest of the ingredients in a gallon-size Ziploc bag and marinate in the refrigerator overnight, turning the bag once or twice. Next day, place tenderloins with marinade in a casserole dish and bake in the oven at 350 degrees for about 1 hour until the tenderloins are done, basting often. Prepare glaze in a large frying pan. Melt sugar in Malta. Add four tablespoons of the marinade. Simmer until the glaze is thick enough to stick to the meat. Turn the heat down low and turn the tenderloins in the frying pan, pouring glaze over them, until well coated. Serve at once.

Black Beans and Rice (Moros y Christianos)

This is Alina's version of the Cuban classic called Moors and Christians.

Serves 8

2 (15-ounce) cans El Ebro black beans
2 cups uncooked rice
1 small bottle of water (500 milliliters)
4 strips bacon, chopped
1 clove garlic, mashed
1 teaspoon salt
⅓ cup olive oil
1 pinch of black pepper
1 pinch of cumin

Cook everything together in a rice cooker or regular covered pot until rice is done, about 20 minutes.

Mojo Sauce

Serve hot over yuca, potatoes, cabbage, squash, or any warm vegetable.

½ cup olive oil
6 cloves garlic, mashed with ½ teaspoon salt
1 pinch of black pepper
1 pinch of cumin
Juice of 1 lime

Heat olive oil in a skillet. Add everything. Simmer for a few minutes. Garlic should still be white.

Haute Cajun

*"I don't really like stuffy cooking.
If you feel like putting licorice in the stew
and that tastes good, then that's fine."*

GOLDEN RICHARD STAYS OUT OF TROUBLE BY MAKING ROUX HIMSELF:
"I didn't really cook until I left New Orleans and went to grad school in Columbus, Ohio. Then it sort of dawned on me what I had taken for granted, all these cheap foods, po-boys for three dollars and red beans and rice. So I tried to figure out how to re-create this stuff. The serious problem that I found immediately was ingredients. Things like tasso and andouille and all the meats that are here can't be found. Tasso is like the king of smoked or preserved meat, it's just godly; you can make anything out of it. Same thing with andouille; real andouille is fat, stiff, and fiery hot. It should hurt to eat it. I went to the supermarkets and tried to buy shrimp, and I was appalled to find out that they were sold *each* in Columbus. Frozen little ice blobs for twenty-five cents each, while I remember fresh shrimp being sold for two dollars a pound.

"My dad, before he became a trailer bachelor and hid out in the woods of Abita Springs, was actually a pretty reasonable Cajun cook, so I got some ideas for dirty rice and jambalaya from him. We were very poor, so there was no idea whatsoever of any highbrow cuisine or eating away from home. Everything was very basic. My father moved to New Orleans from Lake

Golden George Richard III

BORN
1964 in Jennings, Louisiana

NEIGHBORHOOD
Irish Channel
(Lakeview pre-Katrina)

OCCUPATION
Professor of computer science

HOLY TRINITY
Olive oil, thyme, onion

FATHER-SON BONDING?
Winn-Dixie Sundays

Golden makes tasso fried rice in five minutes by throwing his wok on the propane burner outside, which he refers to as his "crawfish cooker."

Arthur when I was about five. That's a fairly hardcore Cajun area. They're crazy about everything they can hunt, essentially. Fishing all the time.

"When I was a child I fished a lot. In the parks, like Audubon Park. We dragged home tons of catfish and bass to fry at my grandmother's house. And I used to be a turtle bounty hunter for my dad. He would pay us, I think it was a dollar a pound, to go and catch the soft-shell turtles that live in Audubon Park. This is the standard turtle for making turtle sauce piquante and turtle soup. Now I don't hurt turtles. We've come to an agree-

ment. Maybe it's restitution because my dad just grabs the hacksaw and starts hacking the turtle's head off without killing it or anything, so yeah. That had to stop.

"We took my dad to the zoo and the aquarium, and many people would look at an animal and remark on its color or its mannerisms or something, and my dad, every remark is, 'Yep. Ate one of those.' He's basically eaten everything in the zoo, except for giraffes and other things that are only in Asia. He's eaten squirrels and possums, all that stuff. I have relatives, if they hit something on the road, it is literally dinner. They just throw it in the back of the car and bring it home and cook it. I also remember the squirrels hanging from the clothesline. The standard thing is to hang them by the tail and then pull the little party suits off of them so their fur just goes 'Shuk!' Red tubes of meat hanging on the clothesline. Squirrel gumbo is very popular. I don't have any memories of eating this, but my dad claims that I have.

"For me, the cooking, I like the process a lot. It's a hobby. People are like, 'Oh, you don't have to cook tonight, you've had a long day,' but I would rather cook than not because I enjoy doing it. So I'm not interested in cheating because it shortens the fun. I'm constantly told that you can make roux with packages and bake roux in the oven so you don't have to whisk this Cajun napalm at high speed on the stove, but I don't really care. I would have to find something else to do if I made the roux in the oven or took it out of the freezer, and that would ultimately involve some other debauchery, so it's better to just make the roux yourself.

"Somewhere along the way, this intuition thing just happened. I think that's kind of the magic ingredient. I wish that would happen with things like playing the guitar. Something just clicks and you start to understand, whereas at the beginning of this thing, when I was a bad cook, everything had to be a recipe and I had no intuition at all.

"This place has taught me that you should never eat crappy food. I mean, there's just no excuse whatsoever. It's raised the standard. I just refuse to eat garbage food at any price level at all. We spend way too much money on food because we like weird ingredients, but with some proper choices you really could afford to eat well. You can almost spend your entire day here doing nothing that's not involving food. Making breakfast, working a little bit, making lunch, working a little bit, making dinner, hanging out with friends and drinking wine and spontaneously making chocolate desserts at midnight. It just teaches you that food is really, really important."

—As told by Golden Richard

Tasso Fried Rice

Golden likes to eat this dish just above room temperature or reheated after a night in the refrigerator. The rice tastes smokier the next day, making it great picnic and party food. Cheap too!

Serves 6

3 cups uncooked jasmine rice
4 cups water
½ teaspoon salt
10 tablespoons canola or peanut oil (same as ⅔ cup)
1 onion, chopped
2 cloves garlic, chopped
3 eggs
½ pound pork tasso, chopped fine (Golden uses Jacob's from LaPlace)
8 tablespoons soy sauce (same as ½ cup)
1 tablespoon sesame oil

Cook rice separately in water and salt in a rice cooker or separate pot to a slightly dry texture. Set aside. Heat oil in a wok over high heat. Stir-fry onion and garlic until onions are translucent. Add eggs and stir for 15 seconds. Add tasso and rice and stir-fry until heated through. Add soy sauce and sesame oil and continue to stir-fry until rice is uniform in color. Allow to cool before serving.

Jalapeño Corn Bread

Golden usually removes the seeds from the jalapeño, which gives the corn bread a subtle flavor and just a hint of spice. For more spice, you can include the seeds. For a different flavor, you can add grated cheddar cheese to the batter. Golden does it either way.

1½ cups flour
1½ cups yellow cornmeal
2 teaspoons baking soda
1 teaspoon salt
5 tablespoons sugar
3 eggs
1¼ cups whole milk
1 jalapeño, chopped
1 cup sweet corn kernels (shaved from cooked corn on the cob, or use frozen sweet corn)
1½ sticks butter, melted

Sift flour and baking soda together into a large bowl. Add cornmeal, salt, and sugar. Blend well. In a separate bowl, lightly beat eggs and then add milk, jalapeño, and corn kernels. Pour wet into dry, adding butter. Stir only until combined. Pour into a greased 9-inch by 9-inch baking pan or a regular loaf pan and bake at 350 degrees until lightly browned, which could take anywhere from 20 to 60 minutes depending on your oven and your pan.

Reincarnated Pecan Cookies

"Grandma used to make these fabulous round pecan cookies to die for, and I remember her making, every Christmas, like a hundred dozen cookies, just insane amounts. The family would contribute ingredients, and she'd spend all her time in the kitchen cranking this stuff out. These particular ones she had to hide. They just evaporated. So I spent about a day just making batch after batch, just based on intuition of what was in them. Finally we had a lot of really great sets of cookies that were not hers because they turned out flat or chewy or something. These were hard and round. Eventually, out comes her cookies from the oven, and that was a monumental moment because now I have a way of having those cookies again. She died in 1999, so there was plenty of opportunity for getting the recipe. You just don't get around to getting it, and then it's too late." Nuts have a lot of oil but no nuts are the same. If you're generous with them and they happen to be oily, you might need as much as 2¼ cups of flour. Since you can add but not take away, start with 1¾ cups of flour and then add more if you can. The dough should be dry and hard but still form balls. Pecans are easily ground in a food processor.

Makes about 40 cookies

2 sticks unsalted organic butter
1 cup sugar
1 tablespoon vanilla
1 dash of salt
2 cups flour (more or less)
2 cups pecan halves, finely ground

Beat butter, sugar, vanilla, and salt until smooth. Mix in flour and ground pecans to make dry dough. Roll into 1-inch balls and place on cookie sheets. Bake at 350 degrees until lightly golden, about 20 minutes. Remove and roll immediately in powdered sugar. Cool, then store in airtight containers.

Back for More

"Sometimes you hit, sometimes you miss. It's jazz cuisine."

ESQUIZITO ACQUIRED A TASTE FOR NEW ORLEANS THOUGH HIS CREOLE FAMILY IN CALIFORNIA: "Welcome to Music Street. Whenever I get a pot of food going, I get in a good mood. Because it's a creative endeavor, and I get into that creative zone where there's a sense of the subconscious coming through, you know. Perhaps I'm receiving messages on how much to put in the food, how to prepare it, different variations, like from some other place, like maybe my ancestors, or something. Or maybe there is a spirit of cuisine in New Orleans, you know. If you open yourself up to it, it hits you.

"I guess I learned to cook by watching my mother and my sister and to some degree my father, but basically I'm self-taught. Self-taught through traditional practices.

"I was the only one in my family not born in New Orleans. I was born in Los Angeles. I'm the baby of the family. I've been here as a resident, sure enough, since late '98.

"I grew up eating red beans and rice on Saturdays, which I guess was my grandmother's tradition. Saturdays was like the traditional washday. Sunday was a meat day, and on Monday you ate leftover meat. I grew up eating New Orleans food but also, my mother, maybe she wanted to expose us to differ-

Eric Paul "Esquizito" Perez

BORN
1963 in Los Angeles, California

NEIGHBORHOOD
Downtown

OCCUPATION
Musician

HOLY TRINITY
Garlic, cayenne, Creole mustard

EATS HIS CEREAL?
In Blue Lu Barker's bowl!

Esquizito learned from a friend how to cook in cast-iron pots over hot coals in his backyard. A steady stream of rum cocktails under the banana trees makes the experience even more satisfying.

ent ways of being, like she would make things like Polynesian chicken or something, which was of course not really authentic but it was something exotic that she wanted to try her hand at, I guess.

"My mother was interested in exposing her children to a broader world than what New Orleans could offer. I think she was the motivation for moving the family out of New Orleans. They left in the late 1950s, and there was still a great deal of turmoil down here so that was primarily their desire, to get away from that and also provide for better opportunities for us, their children.

"You have to understand, there was a great migration of New Orleans people in the 1950s. Mostly to California and specifically to Los Angeles. So there was a whole New Orleans community that just kind of stayed close-knit. All of my mother's side of the family lived in Los Angeles. It was like growing up in a New Orleans environment, because of the people, that's what gave me a sense of what New Orleans was about, even

though it was in Los Angeles. There wasn't a sense that New Orleans was all that far away. Geographically even.

"There was a sausage maker from the Seventh Ward, Sonny Vaucresson. Sonny would come to Los Angeles with a shipment of sausage and hogshead cheese. He'd meet up at somebody's house and the telephone grapevine would start. 'Oh, Sonny's in town.' They'd all go over there and they'd buy some sausage and hogshead cheese. Or somebody would come visit and they'd bring back a big ice chest of shrimps and oysters. My father used to do that; he used to bring it on the plane, checked luggage. New Orleanians are very particular about their shrimps, you know, and it was also a lot cheaper to do it that way. It was just an organic, natural process.

"I think there was a need for them to be who they were. New Orleans culture is so strong that just if you're away from the city, it still is going to be a force in your life, which I find now, the situation that many New Orleanians are in, not being in the city since Katrina, perhaps they're going through the same things that my parents went through, being away from the environment that they grew up with and loved and needless to say, not everything about New Orleans then or now was lovesome.

("Let me go check on this chicken and rice.)

"New Orleanians are very expressive people. Everything they do has this element of personal self-expression to it. And it permeates cuisine. I fit in just fine because I don't follow a recipe; I just kind of consider it jazz cuisine. It's different every time. I do something else to it, like this I made with coconut milk and curry, for a different flavor, but I didn't put a whole lot of curry in it so it's not predominantly a curry chicken. But I'm always, again, maybe even drawing from a subconscious place. That's what makes it interesting to me. It's a creative process. Like here, I was hoping for more pepper, but those red peppers weren't as potent as I thought. I'm still, I consider all of this trial and error, you know. This pot could have used more salt. Just this process of self-crit. I couldn't say that there was definitely, looking back on

it, any evolutionary path other than just a sense of improvisation. You find that in music and in cuisine. That search for freedom, more freedom, you know. The people played the music not in the way necessarily that they were taught but they gave it their own expression that allowed them to feed their souls best. It seems like that happens with food because food in New Orleans is a sensual experience, it's another pleasure of life. So it just leads individuals to want to create with the medium of food, seems to me.

"If I didn't cook, what would be my alternative? I'd have to eat out, and as a musician I decided long ago that I would cook for myself always. If I didn't have a whole lot of money, I'd still make sure that I ate well.

"It's been said that as a musician, now in New Orleans, every note counts, and I think for foodies and cooks, every meal counts."

—*As told by Esquizito*

Singing About Food

Food is a common theme in New Orleans and Louisiana songs, often used as a double entendre for other things. There are hundreds of songs to listen to while you cook, and here are a few:

"I've Got the Yes We Have No Bananas Blues" by Eva Taylor accompanied by Clarence Williams's Blue Five (Okeh, 1923)

"The Frim Fram Sauce" by Louis Armstrong & Ella Fitzgerald (Decca, 1946)

"Hey la bas" by Celestin's Original Tuxedo Orchestra (DeLuxe, 1947)

"Chili Sauce" by Louis Prima with Keely Smith (Breaking It Up, Columbia, 1952)

"Hot Cross Buns" by Paul Gayten (Chess King of New Orleans, Chess, 1959)

"Jambalaya" by Professor Longhair (Rock 'n' Roll Gumbo, Dancing Cat, 1985)

"Save the Bones" by Danny Barker (Save the Bones, Orleans, 1988)

"Cabbage Head" by Dr. John (Goin' Back to New Orleans, Warner Bros, 1992)

"Red Beans" by Marcia Ball (Blue Horse, Rounder, 1994)

"Who Stole the Hot Sauce" by Chubby Carrier (Too Hot to Handle, Louisiana Red Hot, 1999)

"Tomato Song" by Sunpie Barnes (Sunpie, Louisiana Red Hot, 2001)

Sweet Potato Smoothie

Make sure all ingredients are very cold, since there is no ice in this recipe. Esquizito usually prepares this for breakfast.

Yields 2 large servings

1 large sweet potato (steamed, peeled, cut into chunks, and frozen)
1 banana (peeled, cut into chunks, and frozen)
2 cups soymilk
½ cup vanilla yoghurt
1-inch slice soft tofu
2 tablespoons peanut butter
2 tablespoons maple syrup or honey
1 cup cold coffee (optional)
2 ounces Amaretto (optional)

Mix everything in a blender until smooth. Pour into chilled glasses. Enjoy.

Curry Coconut Chicken and Rice

This is a delight of a one-pot meal, simple and satisfying. The dish becomes extra special when cooked over hot coals, which gives it a paella feeling—something interesting happens with the rice—and a hint of smokiness. Resist adding more coconut milk, as the rice can get quite oily. The water amount in this recipe is based on the cooking being done over hot coals. If you put it in the oven, the coconut milk and the water should together amount to little more than 4 cups.

Serves 6

6 chicken thighs
2 tablespoons olive oil
2 cloves garlic, crushed
2 teaspoons Tony Chachere's Creole Seasoning
1 yellow onion, thinly sliced
2 cloves garlic, pressed
1 teaspoon crushed bay leaf or 4 whole bay leaves
1 tablespoon curry powder
¼ teaspoon cayenne
2 cups uncooked rice
¾ cup coconut milk
4 cups water

In a Dutch oven on the stove or in a cast-iron pot over hot coals: Fry chicken thighs in olive oil skin side down with crushed garlic and Tony's until almost all the way done. Remove chicken from pot; cool, and then remove skin from chicken. Brown the yellow onion in the oil left in the same pot. Add pressed garlic, bay leaf, curry powder, cayenne, and rice. Toast the rice for a few minutes before adding water and coconut milk. Last, add the chicken. Bring to a boil, cover, and cook for 30–40 minutes either over hot coals or in a 350 degree oven. Check after 15–20 minutes to see if there is liquid left in the pot. If not, and the rice is still hard, add ½ cup of water.

Bread Pudding with Government Fruit

"Am I down to my last government fruit cup?!" he asked, reaching into his pantry exactly one year after Hurricane

Katrina brought disaster and government fruit to Downtown New Orleans. During evacuation, Esquizito baked bread pudding in Brooklyn, New York, as a way of making his stay in a guest room at a public relations firm more agreeable to the employees. "The first thing they asked was, 'Can he cook?' So I made them this bread pudding first off. And they were impressed with that so I said, 'This is going to be easy.'" At home, he prefers to bake it in a cast-iron pot over hot coals in his backyard.

Serves 12

¾ loaf French bread

6 eggs

1 cup sugar

2½ cups milk

½ teaspoon salt

1 tablespoon ground cinnamon

½ teaspoon ground nutmeg

3 ounces Amaretto or Appleton dark rum

3 (4-ounce) mixed fruit cups (or same amount canned fruit, drained and cubed)

½ cup raisins, presoaked in the Amaretto or rum

1 tablespoon oil or butter

Tear or cut bread into pieces and dry it out on a cookie sheet in the oven if not already dry. Whisk eggs and sugar together in a bowl. Add milk, salt, cinnamon, nutmeg, and Amaretto. Grease your baking dish or pot. Layer bread, egg mixture, mixed fruit, and raisins, ending with egg mixture. Press down bread to soak everything well. Bake over hot coals, or in the oven at 350 degrees for about 45 minutes until golden.

How to Cook over Hot Coals

You can cook and bake almost anything over hot coals outside, which is a blessing when you don't want to heat up the kitchen. Build a fireplace in your backyard with bricks, or use your regular barbecue pit. Light the coals on fire the way you would for a barbecue, and let the fire begin to die down before you get your pot and start cooking. What pot? Cast iron, preferably. Well seasoned, with a lid. If you don't have a lid for your pot, you can use any all-metal lid that fits. The lid should not have wood, glass, plastic, or rubber parts that can crack or melt. You can also use a cast-iron frying pan as a lid. You control the heat by changing the distance between the coals and the pot. Your pot should sit on a rack about 6 inches above the coals (if you build your own fireplace you can use your oven rack) and not directly on the coals, unless the coals are dying and your food has not finished cooking. If you can't do anything about the distance between the coals and the pot, you can lower the heat by moving some coals off to the side or increase the heat by adding pieces of wood, which will burn, to the coals. With rice dishes and anything that is supposed to boil first and then simmer, make sure you have plenty of heat in the beginning. After boiling starts, cover the pot and lower the heat. For baking, you will need to put coals on top of your pot; the lid should fit tightly or go over the rim of the pot so you don't end up with coal in whatever you're making. If the lid sits close to the food, have less coal on top than on bottom. If the lid sits far from the food, have more coals on top. Because of the intense heat coals give, and depending on how tightly the lid fits the pot, you might need a little bit more liquid than usual in your recipe. Trial and error is the way to find out.

Confections of Faith

*"I make gumbo like they're making over here.
Not like somebody dreaming in Italy."*

GETTING IT RIGHT IS SACRED TO ESTELLA MANTIA: "I came here three days before my twenty-second birthday, so I was almost twenty-two. My husband found out I was American citizen because my mother was American citizen, in Italy. She never gave up her American citizenship. I do things different, because my mother was different than the others. Yes, she was in Italy, but her mind, her basic things, was American. She had American books, that was important. I have Dante here. My mother was in Italy and was American. I am over here and I'm Italian. Because I went to school over there. She went to school over here. So, what did she have, she had Shakespeare. I don't have a Shakespeare over here. I have Dante Alighieri.

"My mother was making apple pie, I grew up my whole life eating apple pie. But they don't know in Italy, apple pie. Cupcakes, my mother used to make like this [hands working fast]. Like nothing.

"When we came over here, I didn't know too much about cooking. I made so many mistakes. But my husband said, 'Try to think of what you did wrong and start all over again.' It was the only way we could have food the way we grew up. It's still the only way for me. I get the recipes from over there. And the first time it's not right, but the second or third time, then I'm sure."

Estella Francesca Cirincione Mantia

BORN
1935 in Alia, Sicily, Italy

LIVES IN
Metairie

OCCUPATION
Homemaker

HOLY TRINITY
Olive oil, cheese, tomato

ESPRESSO?
Yes, but only with company

"When we were baking for St. Joseph this year, we messed up one batch of sesame cookies, because one woman was doing the eggs and the sugar and everything, then somebody else measured the sugar again and put it in the mixer and I came, I didn't know, I said 'Let me put the sugar,' so I put sugar again. The cookies taste good. I'm going to say it's a new recipe. Every year it's the same story. They never learn! For the St. Joseph altar, I want everything perfect, and guess what! Nothing is perfect.

"I learned about St. Joseph altars over here. I didn't know they had St. Joseph altars in Sicily. You know why? Some people with money were doing all this, maybe two in my town, for the

Preparing for St. Joseph's Day, Estella bakes over twenty thousand cookies with the Italian Cultural Society of Greater New Orleans and her granddaughters, Leigh-Ann, Kelsey, and Marisa Naccari. Estella stores all the cookies in her garage and suffers nightmares about burglaries.

poor, poor people. My father did not allow me to go over there, even to look. Because it was a different level, it wasn't my class to go over there.

"I cook modern Sicilian. I don't use that strong, heavy, red gravy. Everything is light, and nice, and fresh. Sicilian cooking is different now. The thing is, they use too much garlic here. In Sicily or in Italy, they don't use all that garlic they put over here. Starting from Emeril and all the chefs down. They say this is Sicilian; this is Italian. We use garlic, but not excessively like over here. It's too much. It takes over the flavor of the other ingredients. And we use fresh basil. Not oregano! Fresh *basil*. They put oregano in everything! They make meatballs and spaghetti and they put basil and they put oregano. The oregano is so strong! It doesn't belong in the meatballs or with the gravy. Why'd you put oregano?

"What do they eat, the American people? All year round the same thing; you go to the grocery, you've got eggplant, cauliflower, broccoli, and string beans. Zucchini, the yellow one, and the green. The same things all year round. In Italy they have seasonal, that's why everything tastes better. Because everything is fresh from the ground or from the tree. And local. You're supposed to wait for things.

"All my grandchildren drink coffee since they were a little baby. When they come and see me, we have coffee and we put a little milk for them, they put the sugar. They sit around nice.

Nonna doesn't want any spill; watch what you're doing! One hand under the table, one hand to hold the coffee. They listen, because otherwise, they're not gonna get coffee. That's how you start educating children. At the table.

"I like the New Orleans food. I don't go out to eat gumbo, because I like my own gumbo. I like jambalaya, but I've got to make my own.

"I do my way. What everybody says, whatever they want to say, I don't pay attention. I know better. So, forget it. I don't get involved. I just shut up. Each town has got its own different way. It's got its own different recipe. Who puts this, who puts that, who doesn't put it—everybody's got something different. I do my way, I don't interfere. I never pay attention when they argue. I do my way and they shut up, and then look . . . I know the way you're supposed to do it. Quality is *important*."

—*As told by Estella Mantia*

The Blessed Table

St. Joseph's Day, celebrated on the nineteenth of March, offers an opportunity to go visit strangers in New Orleans and taste their cooking. Sicilian descendants and other Catholics put their addresses in the local newspaper and open their doors to anyone who wants to drop by to admire their richly decorated altars, grab some lucky fava beans, and enjoy a plate of food. Thanks are given to St. Joseph for preventing a famine in Sicily during the Middle Ages, healing a sick relative, or for saving New Orleans from another hurricane. Everyone has a reason. The altars are usually loaded with food, the most precious of offerings to both Sicilians and New Orleanians. Because St. Joseph's Day falls in Lent, there is no meat on the altars. Among bottles of wine, homemade breads, Bible-shaped and cross-shaped layer cakes, sfingi (Sicilian beignets), fig and sesame cookies, fresh fruits and vegetables, stuffed artichokes and eggplants, there is often a whole baked redfish or a big lobster. Many serve pasta with Milanese sauce, made from anchovies, sardines, fresh fennel, pine nuts, and currants—in tomato sauce, of course—topped with toasted and seasoned breadcrumbs, representing the sawdust of St. Joseph the Carpenter.

Sesame Cookies for St. Joseph

Make sure you roll this dough fairly thin, probably thinner than you think it should be and never thicker than your thumb, since it expands in the oven. You can also add lemon or orange zest for a different flavor. Some New Orleans Italian families add almond extract to their sesame cookies, but Estella is clear: "No almond, *never* almond." She then adds, "I could be your mother, so don't get offended."

Makes about 200 cookies

2 pounds unbleached flour
¼ teaspoon salt
2 tablespoons baking powder
¾ pound vegetable shortening
3 large eggs
2 cups sugar
½ cup milk
2 tablespoons vanilla
2 cups brown sesame seeds

Mix flour, salt, and baking powder in a large bowl. Add shortening, spreading and massaging it into the dry at first and then working out smaller lumps with hands as if you were washing them in flour. In a separate bowl, lightly whisk eggs together with sugar, milk, and vanilla. Add egg mixture to flour mixture, forming dough. Wrap dough in plastic foil and let rest for about 15 minutes. Pour sesame seeds into a strainer and rinse with water. Shake the water out. Divide dough into several equal parts about the size of your fist. Then form long, thin rolls with hands and roll these into plenty of sesame seeds, coating well. Cut the roll straight across or diagonally every 2 inches, forming cookies. Gently tamp cookie ends into sesame seeds and place 1 inch apart on cookie sheets. Bake at 375 degrees for about 20 minutes until golden on top and golden (but not brown) on the bottom.

Fig cookies shaped like baby shoes, which Estella has been saving for years.

Chocolate Cookies for St. Joseph

Estella added chocolate chips to this recipe to please her grandkids, "because they're very spoiled."

Makes about 200 cookies

2½ pounds unbleached flour
¼ teaspoon salt
2 tablespoons baking powder
1 cup unsweetened cocoa
1 pound vegetable shortening
4 large eggs
3 cups sugar
¾ cup milk
2 tablespoons vanilla
2 cups chocolate chips

For glaze:
2 cups confectioners' sugar
1 tablespoon vanilla
3 tablespoons milk
1 pinch of salt

Mix flour, salt, baking powder, and cocoa in a large bowl. Add shortening, spreading and massaging it into the dry at first and then working out smaller lumps with hands as if you were washing them in flour. In a separate bowl, lightly whisk eggs together with sugar, milk, and vanilla. Add egg mixture to flour mixture together with the chocolate chips, forming dough. Wrap dough in plastic foil and let rest for about 15 minutes.

Divide dough into 8 equal parts and then each part into about 25 balls. Place balls on cookie sheets, gently touching each cookie with the palm of your hand to flatten slightly so it stays in place. Bake cookies at 350 degrees for 15–20 minutes, making sure cookies do not turn black on the bottom. Cool. For glaze, stir all ingredients together to a smooth and yoghurt-like consistency. Be careful not to add too much liquid, as the glaze easily becomes too runny. With a stiff brush or your finger, glaze the top of each cookie and then put it back on the cookie sheet or cooling rack so that the glaze can set before the cookies are stored.

Lavish Leftovers

*"I guess I learned to cook from
my mother and Martha Stewart."*

Bobby Skinner

BORN
1959 in New Orleans, Louisiana

NEIGHBORHOOD
Gentilly

OCCUPATION
Piano rebuilder, musician,
retired flight attendant

HOLY TRINITY
Butter, garlic, onion

SECRET INGREDIENT?
Liquid crab boil

BOBBY SKINNER COOKS UP LOTS OF FOOD, FRIENDS, AND FABULOUSNESS:
"Both sides of my family is the typical New Orleans mess. My mother's side is Spanish-Hungarian, actually Hungarian-Jewish, Spanish by way of El Salvador. My grandfather and grandmother had an opera and ballet company, which is how they met, accidentally, in Europe. My father's side is all based here in New Orleans, mostly Irish immigrants who settled in the Irish Channel.

"My mother was very adventuresome with food. She exposed us to everything, which is really pretty fabulous. My father would stick to the traditional New Orleans menu. If there was any red beans and rice, any fried fish or gumbo, my father would provide all of that. My mother tried to short-circuit the New Orleans menu by throwing in chilaquiles, which is a Salvadoran tortilla, a big fat tortilla that is sliced open and stuffed with cheese and then rolled in a batter and fried and then baked with a tomato sauce on top.

"Then, my grandmother continued to make Hungarian pastries. For the holidays she did gypsy's arm, which is basically a jelly roll. Out of this world. There was another one called szilvás gombóc, which is a potato dumpling, and there was a piece of fruit put on the inside with sugar and cinnamon and

After the New Leviathan Oriental Fox-Trot Orchestra's regular gig at Jazz Fest, in which he plays the theremin, Bobby feeds more than fifty people at his house from three large buffet tables. Gretchen Bosworth thanks him with a hug, while his dog, Sweet Pea, searches around for dropped goodies. To the far right, orchestra member John Craft.

then it's rolled and boiled and rolled in breadcrumbs and fried in butter and served with sour cream.

"We had a maid living in the house who was from El Salvador. Paz was the maid's name. My mother and Paz would collaborate on all these Latin American dishes, because a lot of them are extremely labor intensive. Chilaquiles was a perennial favorite, and another one was Salvadoran tamales, which are a big production. They would make two batches, a salt batch and a sweet batch. My mother would make hundreds and stick them in the freezer. The savory ones had olives, capers. The sweet ones had prunes, dates, raisins. I preferred the sweet ones.

When you wrap them up, of course, you don't know what they are. Depending on how many glasses of wine my mother had before she made them, you know, Paz and my mother would start wrapping them and come up with a system, maybe two knots was for sweet ones and a single knot for the salty ones on the string that goes on the outside. They're wrapped up in banana leaves first, and then they're wrapped up with aluminum foil. Once the foil goes on, you have no clue what's inside. There was always a question as to what you were going to get when you went into the freezer, because they forgot how many knots they were supposed to put.

"My favorite dinner parties are often a potluck thing, we do an orphan Thanksgiving and an orphan Christmas where everybody brings leftovers from their families. Leftovers usually sit in the refrigerator until they go bad, but we all get together and drop everything on the kitchen counter and there is just no limit to what the variety is. Just local theater friends and musicians; we all meet at a friend's house and everybody just shows up with stuff. That's one of my favorite things. Everybody goes home with an empty dish so you don't have to feel guilty. Not the fanciest parties, but they tend to be more fun. Food is the basis for the conversations. Everybody wants to know who brought this or who brought that, what's in that and how did you make it? Whose recipe was that? Did your mother make it? Did you make it yourself?

"The culture of passing around recipes is not as much a big thing as passing around little secrets for where to get the best seafood, the best shrimp, or the best ingredients. Or little tricks. Like jambalaya, somebody told me about the Rotel tomato thing a bunch of years ago, and they naturally assumed that I knew how to make jambalaya. I knew, I had been making jambalaya for years, but the Rotel tomato saved me about four steps and a bunch of money because fresh tomatoes are expensive. I used to shy away from using canned anything, but canned tomatoes are a good thing.

"For Mardi Gras, remember, everyone's in costume. I've tried to do barbecue in a costume. It doesn't work. I've tried to do corn on the cob in a costume. That was a disaster. You've got to take half of your costume off to eat it. If you're wearing a cute little Doris Day outfit, you know, with white gloves, you don't want to mess up your gloves. And then you're going to try to eat corn on the cob with your lipstick? I don't think so. Better to do red beans and rice with a spoon or a fork and it's not going to mess up your makeup. Jambalaya or gumbo, standard New Orleans party foods. You can handle a bowl and a spoon. But remember, you have a drink to deal with too."

—*As told by Bobby Skinner*

Queen of All Vegetables

Cabbage was always important in New Orleans cooking. A visitor to the French Market in the 1800s wrote: "Flat white-headed cabbages . . . are placed in long rows above one another on the stall counters where they rest, demure, stolid and uniform in appearance . . . [Men] and women handle the cabbages in a manner more delicate and respectful than that they use toward other vegetables. The bags of potatoes, baskets of beans, bunches of carrots, beets, and other stuffs are pitched unceremoniously on the stands, while numerous humble flat squashes are chucked unostentatiously beneath the stands as if there were no people in the world who had any regard for squash . . ." (*Historical Sketchbook and Guide to New Orleans and Environs*, published by Will H. Coleman, 1885).

Stuffed Mirlitons

"I'll do them for a party but I won't put them in half of a mirliton shell. I take a muffin tin and slice some of the mirlitons and put one or two slices on the bottom of the muffin tin, so people know what it is, and then portion the stuffing out with an ice cream scoop, add some Hungarian sweet paprika on top and then bake them. That's sort of my signature way of doing things. You'll probably eat the portion you get."

Makes 24

2 large muffins tins (12 holes in each)
24 extra large aluminum baking cups (or use aluminum foil to line tins)
8 large mirlitons (each the size of two fists)
1 tablespoon salt
Olive oil
1 cup andouille or smoked sausage, in half-moon slices
2 yellow onions, diced
1 bunch green onions, chopped
1 cup diced celery, with leaves
4 cloves garlic, minced
1 cup diced green bell pepper
1 cup chopped parsley (about 1 bunch)
1 stick butter
Zest of 1 lemon
1 teaspoon salt
1 teaspoon black pepper
2 teaspoons liquid crab boil
2 cups shrimp or imitation crabmeat, in chunks
1 cup shredded sharp cheddar
About 2 cups Italian breadcrumbs
Paprika

In a very large stockpot, boil mirlitons whole until soft (check with sharp knife) for about 1 hour (starting from cold water). Let cool for at least 1 hour. Peel by rubbing mirlitons with hands or use potato peeler. Cut mirlitons in half, "along the butt crack." Remove pits using a soup spoon. Slice 2 mirlitons (4 halves) in ¼-inch slices with a mandoline or by hand. This should make at least 24 nice slices (for presentation). Chop remaining mirliton coarsely and put into a colander over the sink with salt to weep out the moisture for at least 20 minutes. Slice, dice, and chop all remaining ingredients. In a splash of olive oil, sauté the sausage down for 10–15 minutes to render out some of the fat. Add all vegetables (except the mirliton, which should be weeping over the sink) and butter, and sauté this for another 10–15 minutes. Add lemon zest, salt, pepper, and liquid crab boil. Also add the shrimp or crabmeat at this time and cook it for about 10 minutes. Squeeze out most of the liquid from the chopped mirliton in the colander and add mirliton to pot. Heat for 10–15 minutes, and then turn heat off. Fold in cheese and enough breadcrumbs to form a dressing. "Don't beat it up." In muffin tins lined with aluminum baking cups, add one of the pretty slices of mirliton on the bottom and an ice cream scoop of stuffing in each. If you don't have a large mechanical ice cream scoop you can use two spoons. Top with a pinch of paprika. Freeze stuffed mirlitons in muffin tins, then remove from tins and transfer to Ziploc bags until the party. Heat at 350 degrees in the oven for 30–45 minutes in a covered casserole dish with a little water on the bottom. Toward the end, leave the cover off for color. To serve, turn aluminum cups upside down on a plate so the mirliton slices show.

Cabbage Rolls

Great to make with free cabbage caught along the parade route on St. Patrick's Day! "A gift from the gutter."

Serves 8–12

2 heads cabbage
2 cups cooked white rice
1 pound ground chuck
1 pound ground pork
1 cup chopped yellow onion
½ teaspoon ground nutmeg
1 teaspoon salt
1 teaspoon black pepper
2 quarts chunky tomato sauce (Bobby adds 1 tablespoon of
    vinegar and 2 tablespoons of sugar to each quart)

Remove tough and dirty outer leaves from cabbages. Remove stems by cutting a wedge about 4 inches in. Place cabbages, 1 at a time, in a very large stockpot with 1 inch boiling water. Cover and let steam for about 10 minutes until outer leaves feel papery (neither brittle nor mushy). Place steamed cabbage on a kitchen towel, being careful not to pierce or bruise leaves. Peel off 4–6 outer leaves, then return cabbage to pot and continue to steam until more leaves can be removed without breaking. Repeat until you have at least 24 good-sized intact cabbage leaves. Shred inner leaves that are too small to stuff and use this to cover the bottom of a deep glass or porcelain casserole or Dutch oven dish (with lid). Remove stems from stuffing leaves with kitchen scissors (cutting a V). Mix the stuffing (from rice to black pepper) in a bowl. Place about ¼ cup of stuffing shaped into a small log at the top of the V. Fold two cabbage flaps diagonally over stuffing, then roll the whole thing once. Fold in sides (like a burrito) and then roll the whole way up. Continue stuffing leaves until there is no stuffing left. Place cabbage rolls seam side down on shredded cabbage in the casserole dish. Pour the first quart of tomato sauce over the first layer, add a second layer of cabbage rolls, and top with the second quart of tomato sauce. Cover dish with lid, leaving a crack for steam to escape, and bake in the oven at 350 degrees for about 1 hour until stuffing is fully cooked. Place a cookie sheet under the dish to catch tomato overflow.

Discriminating Tastes

"You never cook the same pot twice."

Beulah Kenney Labostrie

BORN
1921 in New Orleans, Louisiana

NEIGHBORHOOD
Seventh Ward

OCCUPATION
Homemaker

HOLY TRINITY
Onion, garlic, green onion

FILÉ GUMBO?
Never in summer!

BEULAH LABOSTRIE GREW UP IN A CREOLE FAMILY THAT ENJOYED MUSK-RAT, BUT NEVER RACCOON: "I came from what they call the Seventh Ward. And that ward had a society of its own, where the people had things in common. Their religion, their color, different things made them a special people. And since they were all together, the social life and the foods all blended naturally. Grandmother cooked, Mother cooked, and the children copied. I think a lot of this cooking evolved from the social part because they had gatherings when it was all about eating. It was a banquet, but they called it a *banquet* [bon-KAY] because a lot of people spoke French. All year round, *banquets*, and the good cooks all cooked and brought their special foods to see who could cook these things best. It grew from that. You ate something and then you could go home and duplicate that and cook that same thing too. It wasn't so difficult because most of the people knew the same form of cooking.

"You ate what was available. In the area we lived there were truck gardens right in your neighborhood. We had people from Europe, Czechoslovakia, Italy. Things we ate they grew. If there wasn't one right around you, they had men with wagons who bought it from them and peddled it in the neighborhoods.

Beulah celebrated her eighty-fifth birthday with "not so many, about a hundred" family members. These are some of the women in the family who came.

Cabbage and fresh greens, okra in okra season, tomatoes, egg-plants, parsley, green onion. Even orange potatoes, sweet potatoes, all that was grown right in your neighborhood. I don't know why they were called truck gardens. It really was just an urban gar-den. Truck gardens, I guess, because they trucked it to the French Market, and then the peddlers got it and brought it to us.

"We had a lot of seasoning in everything, that's another thing we had. We didn't like pepper so much like they say, but we liked seasonings. You put bay leaf, and, of course, you had

onion and garlic and green onions and parsley and thyme and then maybe some oregano. We didn't eat hot. That was not our group. That's a Cajun thing. Everything had to be almost mild, mild tasting.

"Rice was a basic; you ate rice every day. Most we ate rice. We cooked potatoes now and then, but we would smother them down in a frying pan with smoked sausage or just onions. You could feed your children these potatoes. With rice, of course.

"I love to cook. I never did not want to cook. I wanted to give my family the best I could. But I always believed in keeping some money for a rainy day. You don't eat all this high stuff today because you can't feel it tomorrow. I'd rather eat beans every day than gumbo today and nothing tomorrow.

"We ate a lot of liver. We all liked liver. We used to eat cow brains, all kinds of things people don't eat now. It was a delicacy for those who liked it and knew how to fix it. Oh Lord, I fixed it. My children still talk about it. 'Mama, when are you going to cook those cow brains?' You had to clean it, of course, which was tedious. You had to get all the little veins off the brain. Put salt and pepper, put it in cornmeal and fry it. It was delicious. Another thing we ate a lot was cow tongue. We baked it and made it like a roasted tongue. You could use it for lunch.

"When I was a little girl and we lived in Slidell, the people there were mainly Mississippians. My mother was from New Orleans. She didn't adopt no country cooking. My mother never made a biscuit. She didn't know how to make corn bread. We sent to the French bakery and bought French bread because that's what we knew. She didn't adopt a thing. They ate this fat-back and biscuits, while my mama wouldn't have dared fry that. If I wanted to eat fatback or biscuits or corn bread, I had to go to one of my friends' houses. My mother was a city person.

"Muskrat, before the nutria came, occupied the swamps between New Orleans and Slidell, and my mother would cook muskrat. Them people wouldn't have dared cook that. They'd say, 'Uh, I wouldn't eat that. That's a rat.' But the New Orleans people knew how to eat different things. Now, those country people ate possum, coons. My mother wouldn't eat that. She didn't like that, though, you see? She didn't care for that. She would eat rabbit, but she didn't care for possum or coon. They're all the same animals in a sense, but these are the different ideas you've got about what's good, bad, or whatever.

"I was never a recipe person. I never looked at a recipe in my life. Never, never. No! I would ask somebody, 'How do you make that?' And then I'll go try it, experiment some kind of way until I get it the way I want it. I never used a recipe in my life."

—*As told by Beulah Labostrie*

Not Just Hot

When you say "seasonings" in New Orleans, you mean a lot more than cayenne, thyme, oregano, salt, and pepper. You mean yellow onion, bell pepper, and celery (the standard "holy trinity") as well as garlic, green onions, and fresh parsley. When a New Orleanian says "highly seasoned" or "plenty, plenty seasonings," he or she is not necessarily referring to the spice level of a dish, but to ingredients otherwise known as *vegetables*. There is no question that many locals enjoy hot, spicy food. But New Orleans home cooking is not always as spicy as many people think. Its reputation for spiciness might to some degree rest on a misunderstanding of the local parlance, where "seasonings" belong in the produce section.

Filé Gumbo

Sunday dinner without gumbo was unthinkable for most of Beulah's life, "even insult." She made okra gumbo from March to October, and from October to March she made filé gumbo. "Seafood was always available. There was no time when you didn't have seafood. In the winter we made filé because it would sour very quickly in the heat. We didn't have refrigeration and the house was very hot, so you didn't fool with the filé gumbo in the summer because it was difficult to keep it from souring. Okra wouldn't do that. The okra didn't sour like that. Very dangerous to eat, filé gumbo in summer." Beulah likes her roux nice and dark, "a deep nut brown, almost burnt!" Her recipe for good roux includes patience and a good iron frying pan. She always serves her gumbo with French bread and beer. (Author's note: This was the first time I had ever used chicken necks. On the advice of a fellow shopper at Dorignac's, I boiled them in a separate pot of water until tender for about 30 minutes. I then strained and saved the liquid, which I later added to the gumbo as part of the water. I also removed the skin from the cooled chicken necks before I added them with the rest of the meats to the gumbo. You can also add them raw to the gumbo, if you first remove the skin. Beulah says to do it either way. I also found that the gumbo tasted its absolute best on the third day. The gumbo has a wonderfully herby taste thanks to all the parsley and filé, and it becomes smokier as it sits, thanks to the sausage.)

Serves 24

4 big cooking spoons vegetable oil (about ½ cup)
4 big cooking spoons flour (about ½ cup)

Oil for sautéing
2 yellow onions, diced
1 bunch parsley, chopped (yes, lots!)
1 bunch green onions, chopped
1 head garlic, minced
1 pound veal stew meat, in large cubes
1 container chicken necks (about 1 pound)
1 container chicken gizzards (about 1 pound)
½ pound ham, in cubes ("just meat" seasoning ham—not the sliced kind in salty brine)
1 pound hot smoked sausage, sliced or diced
1 tablespoon thyme
1 tablespoon oregano
4 bay leaves
1 pound shrimp, peeled
7–8 gumbo crabs, split
1 container oysters, with liquid (about 1 pound)
Cayenne to taste (¼ teaspoon or more)
Salt to taste (about 1 teaspoon)
4 tablespoons filé powder

Start by making roux. Heat oil in a cast-iron skillet and stir in flour. Turn the heat down low and stir constantly until the roux becomes dark brown. This should take about 30–40 minutes. In a 12-quart pot, sauté onion, parsley, green onions, and garlic in oil. Add roux and all the meats (but not the seafood) and dry herbs. Fill pot to a little more than half with water. Bring to a boil and simmer for at least 1 hour. Add seafood. Simmer for 10–20 minutes. Add cayenne and salt to taste. Turn the heat off. Add filé. Serve over Louisiana long-grain rice.

Catfish Court Bouillon

When Beulah was coming up, everybody she knew made this dish with catfish heads. But Beulah's husband "couldn't stand no eyes looking up at him," so she switched to fillets. Her court bouillon is really a fish stew, not unlike her shrimp Creole.

Serves 4

¼ cup vegetable oil
¼ cup flour
1 yellow onion, diced
½ cup chopped green onion
2 cloves garlic, minced
1 (28-ounce) can whole tomatoes
2 bay leaves
1 teaspoon thyme
1 teaspoon oregano
Salt to taste
1 pound catfish or redfish fillets, in serving-size pieces
¼ bunch parsley, chopped

Make a light brown roux in a cast-iron skillet by heating oil and stirring in flour. Turn the heat down low and keep stirring until roux has the same color as light brown sugar, about 15 minutes. Add yellow onion, green onion, and garlic, and sauté for a few minutes. Add tomatoes with juice, bay leaves, thyme, and oregano. Cover and simmer for at least 30 minutes. Salt to taste. Add fish and parsley. Simmer for 10 minutes. Serve with rice.

Stuffed Eggplant

This is a mellow, family-friendly side dish and a good accompaniment to attention-seeking main dishes. Beulah made it for family gatherings for over 40 years. "I'm an eggplant person."

Serves 8

2 eggplants
Salt
Olive oil or other fat
1 yellow onion, diced
2 cloves garlic, minced
½ cup chopped green onion
½ pound ham, diced "as small as possible"
½ pound fresh shrimp, peeled and cut in half
½ cup breadcrumbs
Butter

Peel eggplants and cut into ½-inch cubes, removing the seediest parts. Boil in salted water until tender, 15–20 minutes. Drain. Sauté onion, garlic, and green onion in olive oil or other fat. Add shrimp and ham. Add eggplant and breadcrumbs. Mix well and bake in a buttered casserole dish at 350 degrees for about 30 minutes.

The Bean Man

"Heavy, heavy Creole flavor."

CHARLES ALLEN'S MOST CHERISHED INHERITANCE IS HIS RECIPE FOR RED BEANS AND RICE: "I grew up eating filé and okra gumbo, red beans and rice, crawfish bisque, shrimp Creole, crawfish étouffée, fried fish, fried shrimp, fried oysters, fried turkey, fried duck. I grew up eating, some mornings, thanks to my maternal grandfather, I grew up eating fried perch with grits and eggs and toast and coffee. That was our mainstay; fried perch for breakfast.

"At a young age I was drinking coffee. I might have had my first cup when I was seven or eight years old with my maternal grandmother as well as her mother, my great-grandmother. We called her Grams. She was a good cook for red beans and rice. That goes into my story of red beans and rice, the people that really influenced my red beans and rice. First and foremost it's her. Every Mardi Gras day of every year that would come around, she would prepare red beans and rice and fried chicken, and she would cook so much of it for family members as well as neighbors and friends from the neighborhood. She lived in the Lafitte housing project on the corner of Claiborne Avenue and Lafitte Avenue, underneath the overpass. She was there for years, going into seventy years ago.

Charles Edward Allen III

BORN
1973 in New Orleans, Louisiana

NEIGHBORHOOD
Holy Cross

OCCUPATION
University administrator

HOLY TRINITY
Garlic, cayenne,
Tony Chachere's Creole Seasoning

LOVE?
Leftovers!

Charles Allen lives alone but cannot cook for fewer than ten or twelve.

"In the springtime, my grandfather would buy a whole mess of boiled crawfish, and we would eat the crawfish at the kitchen counter, and my grandmother would clean the shells and take some of the meat and make crawfish bisque. That was a big long Friday event. We would start eating crawfish at maybe three or four and she would start cooking at about five. Maybe by ten or eleven o'clock at night you could taste the beginning of it. It was so good. Black New Orleans homes, usually around Easter time, there would be a few evenings when people would be enjoying crawfish bisque. And this is one of the unfortunate things; when she died, we never got her recipe. There are a lot of times my mother and I reflect on that. We never got her recipe for crawfish bisque. And I have not ever tried to use someone else's recipe or experiment on my own. I've been meaning to do that, but I'm fearful of making a big mistake of it all. She made the best crawfish bisque, and she was known for it. I remember she used to say, 'The roux, have it a nice, dark consistency.' She was always a stickler for 'don't

overdo the breadcrumbs because then it just tastes like bread stuffed in the heads,' and that just doesn't taste too well to us. She would make the largest pot of it she possibly could. Make it last a while.

"We call my grandmother *Grandmá.* When my mom tastes my cooking, my pot roast or my roast turkey and says, 'Just like *Grandmá's,*' makes me feel good, you know. I'm the holiday cook on my mom's side. And whenever I prepare my red beans and rice, I usually tell my mom because she looks forward to it. My mom can cook, but she doesn't like to cook too much. I love to cook because I love to eat. My grandfather, my mom's dad, he was really a gourmand. This was a man; he was very robust in size. He could go to some of the finest restaurants in the city, a black man, during segregation as well as modern times, and get the best of service. He treated people with utmost kindness and respect; that was to his advantage. If you wanted a good place to eat in the city you could ask him, and he would know. 'And tell them I referred you.'

"*Grandmá*, what else? She made a really good meat loaf. She would wrap it in bacon, put some strips across the top and prepare it either in a tomato sauce or a brown gravy. When I talk about her cooking I really miss her. She was a great cook. She belonged to a club of women in the city. It was a club of good cooks. They could really cook. I will say this, I couldn't tell much of a difference in how they cooked from my grandmother's style of cooking. Those women, let's say each of their gumbos, red beans and rice and so forth, tasted pretty much the same. So that led me to believe, probably each one learned from the other how to do certain things until after a while, they all kind of did things the same way.

"The best meal of my whole life was my grandmother's crawfish bisque. Really. By far. And I would say the last one that she cooked before she died, which was in the spring of 1989, was the best. Really was. The last year of the cold war. And that fall season was when we learned that she was sick with breast cancer. She died in March. And then I never forget, after she passed away, her good friends did a lot of cooking for us, as a favor to her and to us. They brought dishes of all kinds to the repast, basically the dinner after the services, at our home. It really touched our hearts. I can remember eating my meals and not being able to swallow. I was paining with grief. My grandfather, our gourmand, he was enjoying all the food, but deep down inside, he was grieving as well, he just didn't know how to express it.

"I started cooking that spring season after my grandmother's death. The first dish I cooked was red beans and rice. I wanted to show my grandfather that I could help him the way she did.

Red Beans and Ricely Yours

Almost every New Orleanian cooks red beans, it seems. It's easy and cheap New Orleans food. Locals are used to the question "why red beans and rice on Mondays?" Well, at one time, Monday was a washday when you cleaned your church clothes from Sunday. It was easy to boil water for beans and clothes at the same time, and beans could cook for a while without supervision. There might also have been a hambone left over from Sunday dinner. But why do we eat red beans and not some other bean? We can only speculate that their local popularity has something to do with the love for red beans in Haiti and Cuba, which were intimately connected with New Orleans during French and Spanish rule, as well as after the Louisiana Purchase. Between 1809 and 1810, about ten thousand refugees from French St. Domingue (Haiti) came to New Orleans after the Haitian Revolution turned the slave colony into a free, black republic. This doubled New Orleans's population and reinforced everything that was French, African, and Caribbean (non-Anglo, non-American) about the city. Almost all of these immigrants did not come directly from Haiti but had lived many years in exile on Cuba. When Napoleon put his own brother on the Spanish throne in 1808, however, Cuban hospitality came to an abrupt end. Spanish authorities in Cuba expelled the French speakers, made up of about even numbers of whites, free people of color, and slaves belonging to either of the first two groups. Where did they go? New Orleans! Here, they could at least speak their language. Red beans and rice is known as congri in Cuba, while Haitians call their version riz national, riz et pois rouges, or riz et pois collés.

He enjoyed her red beans and rice, and I wanted to basically treat him to a good pot of red beans and rice. I took great pains that afternoon to make it like my grandmother's, and he enjoyed it when he got home. I never forget. He thanked me by just kind of holding my hand as we sat there and ate, and I wanted to cry. It might have been my cooking that moved him to the point of asking me, 'Would you stay here and live with me?' I lived with him for fifteen months until he passed away in 1991.

"As I'm cooking, I think thoughts of, 'I'm glad I can cook for myself. I'm glad I can stand here at the stove and cook. Cook with comfort and ease.' My recipe for red beans and rice hasn't moved in over ten years because I feel like I have perfected the beans to the point where co-workers of mine love my beans. My boss loves my beans. When there's talk of having a party, I'm approached. I'm the bean man. I'm the bean man. I think my grandmother still lives, my great-grandmother Grams still lives, they each still live in their own unique ways through me, through my cooking and through the rest of us."

—As told by Charles Allen

Backyard Crawfish Boil

During spring and early summer in New Orleans, most people will either host or be invited to a crawfish boil. For a large backyard boil, this is what you do, according to Uptown resident Errol Fouquet: Get 1 or several sacks of fresh live crawfish. Fill an 80-quart pot (with basket insert inside, and the whole thing placed securely over a propane burner) halfway with water. Add 2 (26-ounce) boxes of salt, 24 ounces liquid crab boil, 4 bags dry crab boil, ¼ cup ground Chinese red pepper or cayenne pepper, 10 lemons cut in half, 6 yellow onions (cut into quarters), 8 heads garlic (cut in half to expose all cloves in cross section), 1 large bunch celery cut into chunks, 12 bay leaves, and 1 pound smoked sausage cut into 4-inch chunks. Light the burner. While you wait for the water to boil, purge the crawfish. Dump about half a sack of crawfish into a tub or large ice chest. Cover the crawfish with water and ½ box of salt. Let sit for 10 minutes, drain water, and refill. Let sit for 5 minutes, drain water and refill. Once water in pot comes to a rolling boil, taste it. It should be almost too salty to bear and spicy enough to burn your lips. Adjust seasonings, if necessary. Next, add 1 or 2 small bags new potatoes, 4 ears fresh corn cut into 16 small portions, and maybe some artichokes. Boil for 10 minutes. Move basket to purging area. Drain crawfish and then pour them into basket over potatoes, corn, and everything else in there. You can also add some button mushrooms. Carefully lower basket into boiling water. Once water comes back to a rolling boil, set your timer to 3 minutes. After 3 minutes, kill the flame and add ½ small bag of ice. Stir and let crawfish soak for 15 minutes. They will sink as they soak and absorb flavors. Lift basket and allow to drain. Pour crawfish onto large tables covered with newspaper, spreading them out to stop the cooking process. For additional boils, you will need to reinforce seasonings, adding about half of what you originally added, while being generous with the liquid and dry crab boil. When you're out of crawfish, you can parboil some chicken or pork ribs in the same pot for 1 minute, turn off the flame, and let soak for 2 minutes. Then throw meats on the grill.

Red Beans

Charles began using pickled pig parts in the mid-1990s, learning this from his aunt Lietta. The rest of his recipe is an inheritance from his maternal grandmother and great-grandmother. "We feel that if you keep garlic, green onions, and Tony Chachere's seasoning, you have the basic items for anything, really." He does not answer the telephone while sautéing seasonings, because he doesn't want his base to burn. Later he might not answer the telephone for another reason; he takes a nap while the dish simmers.

Serves 10–15

1 pound hot smoked sausage (in ½-inch slices)
1 pound ham steak (in 1-inch cubes)
1 pound pig parts (optional)
1 pound dried red kidney beans (soaked in water overnight)
1 cup vegetable oil
1 tub Creole mix seasonings (or 1 heaping cup chopped yellow onion, ½ cup chopped green onion, 2 tablespoons chopped parsley)
2 tablespoons minced garlic
2 teaspoons Tony Chachere's Creole Seasoning (or more)

If using pig parts, clean them well under running water, then boil for 30 minutes to remove salt, dirt, and grime, rinsing well before you add them to the beans. In a large pot, let the oil get really hot, and then add seasonings and garlic and sauté for 5 minutes. Add Tony's and meats and sauté for 15 minutes. Add beans. Add 2 quarts of water—Charles uses the soaking water.

Bring beans to a slow simmer. If you see beans at the surface during the first 2 hours of cooking, add more water. Beans should cook for 3–4 hours until creamy. You can mush them against the side of the pot to help this process along. Add more Tony's to taste. Serve beans over rice.

Smothered Okra

This recipe comes from Charles's mother, Rosemarie Allen. You can peel fresh tomatoes in a zap by putting them for a few seconds over a gas burner until the skin blisters and turns yellowy.

Serves 4

2 tablespoons olive oil
1 pound okra, washed and sliced
2 large tomatoes, peeled and chopped
1 yellow onion, chopped
1 green bell pepper, chopped
Salt and pepper to taste
1 pound shrimp, peeled and deveined
5 sprigs fresh parsley, chopped

Cook okra slowly in olive oil in a large skillet with the tomatoes, onion, bell pepper, salt, and pepper. Stir and cook, covered, until okra is tender. Add shrimp and parsley and continue cooking for 3–4 minutes, until shrimp turn pink and opaque. Serve over a hot bed of rice.

Boiled Blue Crabs

This recipe came from Charles's friend Arthur Johnson, who recommends also adding 3 pounds large shrimp, 1 pound hot smoked sausage, and 8 pieces corn on the cob to the pot for a true seafood feast. If you'd like to do this, add them to the pot when you turn the fire off. Shrimp, sausage, and corn will be done when the crabs are ready. In the interest of full disclosure, it should be mentioned that Arthur grew up in the Washington, D.C., area, so this recipe has a Chesapeake Bay influence. The seafood will have a very mild flavor. For a different perspective, read the sidebar on backyard crawfish boils.

Serves 8

3 lemons, quartered
3 ribs celery, cut into pieces
3 heads garlic, cut in half crosswise
8 ounces crab boil
Half a 26-ounce box of salt
2 cans domestic beer
2 dozen live large blue crabs

Fill a 40-quart covered pot (with basket insert) to a little less than half with water; turn on the propane. Add lemons, squeezing them as you put them in, celery, garlic, crab boil, salt, and beer. Bring to a rolling boil for 10 minutes. Next, add crabs (in basket) and boil for 10–15 minutes until crabs turn orange and red. Turn off the propane, stir, and let crabs soak for 20 minutes. Bon appétit!

Refrigerator and Freezer Map

People still talk about the food they lost in hurricane Katrina, a testament to the love, money, and work they continue to dedicate to the things they cook and eat. Here is a list of some of the foods our home cooks had in their refrigerators and freezers during the storm. On the next page, you will find a map of the neighborhoods where the home cooks lived before Katrina, and where they live today. All but six (Asare Dankwah, Mayola Brumfield, Golden Richard, Stephen Gergatz and Julianna Bika, Kalpana Saxena, and Snježana Bjeliš) are now back in their pre-Katrina homes, often with brand-new refrigerators and freezers.

Mayola Brumfield 3–4 turkeys, ham, 5–6 pounds shrimp, 5 pounds catfish, pecan pies, sweet potato pies

Bill Murphy pork chops, ground beef, stew meat, 2 roasts, chicken and seafood

Joanne Cieutat 10 pounds shrimp, 5 pounds crabmeat

Numa Martinez plenty of deer meat

Bellazar Wilcox nothing

Jacqui Gibson-Clark lots of fish, alligator, shrimp Creole

Warren Bell 15 pounds shrimp (just deheaded the day before), gumbo, beans and rice

Kalpana Saxena 2 packages crawfish tails, Chinese sausages, Indian spices, pork, nuts, cottage cheese

Tommy Westfeldt ducks and geese

Marietta Herr venison, wild boar roast

Yo Chin	45 pounds mullet, 5–10 pounds shrimp, 10–15 pounds chicken, 12 pounds crawfish	**Kay Fallon**	5 pounds shrimp, chicken, 1 pound blueberries, 1 pound strawberries, wine
Thania Mae Elliott	too much to list	**Peter Cousin**	chickens, beans, venison
Aida Gray	10-12 lobsters, 50–70 pounds shrimp, 20 packs crawfish tails, 4 big cans lump crabmeat, "many, many" lamb chops and a quarter of a deer	**Chin Thi Nguyen**	fish of all kinds, shrimp, chicken, pork, beef, vegetables
		Snježana Bjeliš	many, many pounds oysters, shrimp, meat, vegetables, milk, cheese
Ronald Lewis	pork chops	**Alina Sedlander**	black beans, red beans, spaghetti sauce
Bertin Esteves	not sure—"I had to leave fast"	**Golden Richard**	stinky French cheeses
Maria, Dolores, and Maria Garcia	all kinds of seafood, such as conch and shrimp	**Esquizito**	whole wheat bread, hummus, tofu, alfalfa sprouts
Karen Clark	Greek mastic, blackberry sage jam, small piece of wedding cake from 1989	**Estella Mantia**	6–7 gallons fig marmalade, Italian capers, Italian bitter almonds, Italian sun-dried tomatoes
Jerome Smith	nothing		
Avery Bassich	assorted wines and champagne, quarts of various soups and gumbo, wild game	**Bobby Skinner**	hundreds of stuffed mirlitons, bell peppers, jalapeños and eggplants, 50 pounds shrimp, a couple of turkeys
Julianna Bika and Stephen Gergatz	paprika, yoghurt, salmon, sausages, poppy seed, chestnut puree	**Beulah Labostrie**	1 pound smoked sausage, 2 pounds pork chops, 3 pounds chicken
Asare Dankwah	peanut butter soup	**Charles Allen**	quarts of red beans
Minda Baker	fish, meat, ham		

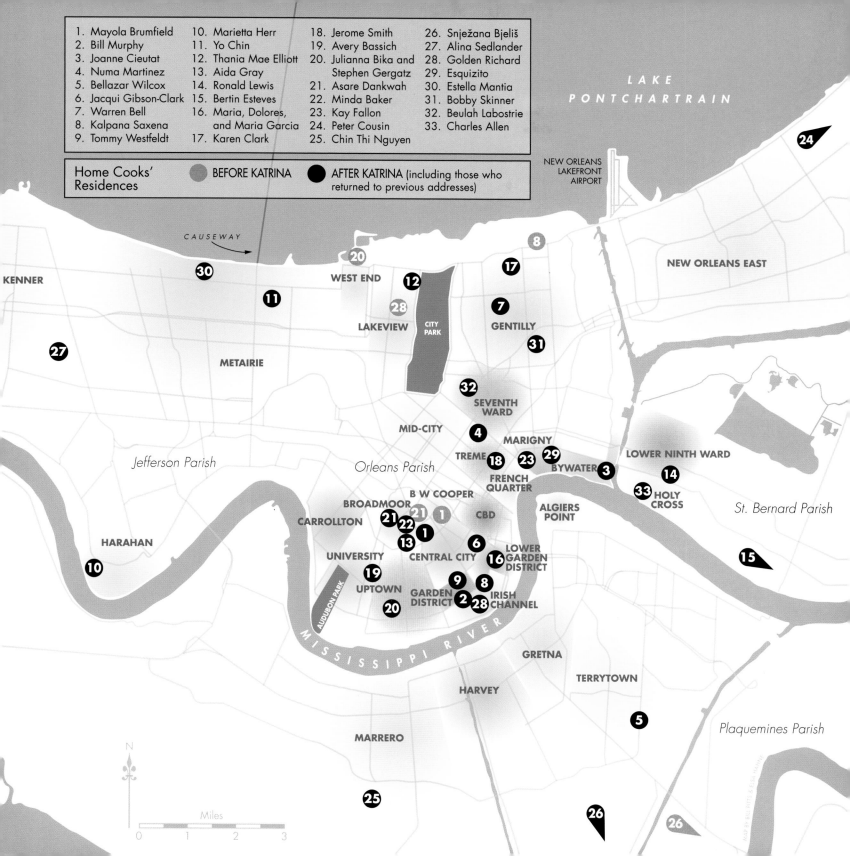

1. Mayola Brumfield
2. Bill Murphy
3. Joanne Cieutat
4. Numa Martinez
5. Bellazar Wilcox
6. Jacqui Gibson-Clark
7. Warren Bell
8. Kalpana Saxena
9. Tommy Westfeldt
10. Marietta Herr
11. Yo Chin
12. Thania Mae Elliott
13. Aida Gray
14. Ronald Lewis
15. Bertin Esteves
16. Maria, Dolores, and Maria Garcia
17. Karen Clark
18. Jerome Smith
19. Avery Bassich
20. Julianna Bika and Stephen Gergatz
21. Asare Dankwah
22. Minda Baker
23. Kay Fallon
24. Peter Cousin
25. Chin Thi Nguyen
26. Snježana Bjeliš
27. Alina Sedlander
28. Golden Richard
29. Esquizito
30. Estella Mantia
31. Bobby Skinner
32. Beulah Labostrie
33. Charles Allen

Home Cooks' Residences ● BEFORE KATRINA ● AFTER KATRINA (including those who returned to previous addresses)

LAKE PONTCHARTRAIN

NEW ORLEANS LAKEFRONT AIRPORT

NEW ORLEANS EAST

CAUSEWAY

KENNER

WEST END

LAKEVIEW

CITY PARK

METAIRIE

GENTILLY

SEVENTH WARD

MID-CITY

Jefferson Parish

Orleans Parish

MARIGNY

TREME

FRENCH QUARTER

BYWATER

LOWER NINTH WARD

St. Bernard Parish

BROADMOOR

B W COOPER

CBD

ALGIERS POINT

HOLY CROSS

CARROLLTON

CENTRAL CITY

LOWER GARDEN DISTRICT

HARAHAN

UNIVERSITY

UPTOWN

GARDEN DISTRICT

IRISH CHANNEL

AUDUBON PARK

MISSISSIPPI RIVER

GRETNA

TERRYTOWN

HARVEY

MARRERO

Plaquemines Parish

N

Miles
0   1   2   3

Recipe Index